Prologue

We are living in exceptional times. Everything is shifting. The people, the animals and the Earth. Life as we have known it is no more. However when one door closes another one opens. Right now we have a choice. We can dwell in the past or prepare for a future.

Choice is the true path to freedom, so which will you choose. This book may help you make the choice to prepare for the future by agreeing to release the parts of yourself that no longer serve you in a positive way. Come with me now into a 5th dimensional reality. A reality where we consciously create as we go along. A reality that is based in love and connection, connection not only to the world around us but to ourselves. Come and experience what it will be like to have ownership of your life without having to fight for your place in society. Feel what it is like to make decisions towards joy while knowing your connection to others will benefit from that decision.

As we consciously step out of the 3rd dimensional reality and into the 5th, let this book help guide you to a new understanding of what reality is. Open up your mind, release your fears, allow yourself to be fully present as the words flow off the pages and into your being. Know that within this world you are welcome, you are loved and you are wanted. Take a few deep breaths and lets get started.

Chapter One

There I was floating in the void. That space that is familiar to all who meditate. The place of nothingness and darkness that brings comfort and peace. That place where you become the blackness that surrounds you. You are nothing and you are everything, and nothing matters except being in that state. It is rare that I achieve that state.

Normally at some point my mind goes rushing off in some direction and I follow it. So those moments that I can steal in eternity are always very precious to me. The moment held me and I was non existing peacefully when I heard a disturbance. Off to my right I could hear something. It sounded like quiet voices on the wind that had been carried a long way. It came with the feeling that something was right there, something I should be seeing, but all I could perceive was the void. Then I felt an energy pulling me ever so gently, increasing in speed taking me from the darkness. There was a pin point of light coming towards me or I to it, I was not sure. As the light came closer the sound got louder. There were voices, many voices, speaking in many languages. I was not sure where I was headed, and then the light consumed me.

As I tried to adjust to the sudden brightness I could see shapes and colours forming around me. I was standing in a large open area on a small knoll overlooking a large field. In the field were thousands of people. They were all dressed in white. Most had gold belts. There were men and women. Some had colourful feathers in their hair. All the people seemed to be indigenous. Distinct facial features led me to believe I was looking at Navaho, Mayan, Tibetan, Toltec and so many other ancient peoples. They were all speaking to one another in their native tongue but they seemed to understand what was being said.

As I looked around, I could see that off to the right there were small temples built on different levels into the hillside. They looked like the images I had seen of the Mayan temples only smaller. There were various other buildings scattered about the landscape and several small standing stones with symbols carved into them. In the centre of the large lawn area was a huge stone table. It was a greyish stone but had a blue tinge at least that is the way it looked from a distance. I did not know where I was. It felt like the places I have been to in Mexico. Lush green foliage everywhere and the air was warm and balmy. As I breathed in the air it seemed to energize me, like it had more oxygen than what I was used to breathing. I was very comfortable here. It felt so familiar to me.

Standing there on that hill it felt like I was trying to remember something that I just could not retrieve. I should know this place but I had no memories of it. Then just as I was trying to grasp on to something that was not there, I saw one of the men by the stone table waving me over. I wasn't sure he meant me, so I looked around but there was no one near me. So I tentatively walked towards the man. Until that very moment I was not completely sure that I was standing in the scene. I thought perhaps I had been brought to this place to see something or to remember something. I wasn't assuming that I was actually part of the landscape.

As I got near the man that had waved me over, I could see him speak to me. In my mind I heard, "Welcome" but his lips did not move in a manner that should have expressed that word. He continued to talk,"We are very happy you found us again. It has been a long journey for you. All your questions will be answered at the time that they are most relevant. Yes you have been here before, but the memories elude you. We are grateful you came home. Would you like to stay?"

It was so weird. Like watching one of those Chinese Kung Foo movies. You hear what they are saying but their lips do not match the words. So surreal. And what did he mean by, "Would I like to stay?" Am I dead? Am I going to die? Not sure how I wanted to answer that. So after many facial contortions, I decided to respond as graciously as I knew how.

"Thank you for your gracious welcome. It is very beautiful here, however I have no idea where I am or what I am doing here?"

All the people in white that heard me broke out in big belly laughs. That actually made me feel better. I didn't feel so much like I was being lured into something if they were laughing at me.

"Forgive us. We thought you had been prepared. Most that come here are ready. You always have done things in an eccentric way, now is no different. You are here in the next world. You would call it the 5th dimension. We are your people. In a past life you were one of us. You worked with the ancient knowledge here in this place.

You loved to work with patterns and disrupted patterns. The proper flow of energy is what you studied. Is any of this sounding familiar to you?"

In my life I do love patterns and I still love to discover a proper flow of energy, but I could not say that I had any memory of what they spoke. I was still getting hung up on the whole words versus lips moving thing. It was just throwing me off. I asked them if they could speak english and they said "No". They however understood me perfectly too, and I had no idea what language they were speaking. They could see that I was spending time trying to figure out why they were the way they were and I was not focusing at all on the message they were trying to send, so they asked me, "Would you be willing to come back again and learn more?"

"Yes", was my instant answer. I loved being in that energy and scenery so much that I would use any excuse to go back. So they told me to come to them the next night, using the same process I had this time. They would find my energy and reel me in so to speak. I agreed and instantly I popped back into my body.

I propped myself up in bed and shook off the residue of the transition. Did that just happen? I really did know better than to ask those questions after all the years and journeys that I have done. Most of the journeys are very different. Usually I go somewhere and watch something, while a distant but clear voice narrates in the background. I see what I have to see and that is it. It is not normal for me to go and interact with a group of people whose words don't match their lip movements. I imprinted my experience into my brain and let it go for the night. Sleep was my goal now, and hopefully not an elusive one.

I did as was asked of me and the very next night I returned. This time when I found myself standing in the field there was a Black Panther there to greet me. I had no fear even though I thought this odd. I knew it was there to escort me for some reason. I went with this majestic being down the length of the field to where the group of people I had previously spoken with were standing.

"Good you are here, are you ready?" He motioned with his hand to move forward as he spoke to me.

"Ready for what?" I responded nervously.

"You have come to finish your initiation into the Jaguar school, have you not?" I could see by the look on his face that he was perplexed. He seemed to think that somehow I knew what I was

5

doing there.

"I have come back because you asked me to come back. I know nothing of this Jaguar anything?" I could hear the fear in my own voice, not knowing what his intentions were and there was still a Black Panther standing beside me.

"Is it not true that many years ago you were in ceremony to own your true nature, the Jaguar nature?" I was not sure how he knew that. It was so many years ago now and I was never sure what had happened was real or not. The circumstances under which I had participated in that ceremony were quite unusual.

"Yes it is true, but I never really believed any of that. It just seemed like I was the centre of some tourist attention. So you are telling me now that it was all real and it was supposed to mean something?" I actually couldn't believe those words were coming out of my mouth now, so many years had passed since that ceremony.

"If you are to fully integrate this medicine you must finish the ceremony. Time does not matter. You have been stuck in time since that ceremony, do you not want to move forward? Do you not want to discover the truth of who you are? If this is not what you are here for, please do not ask us to waste our energy. All of this is for you. You have been waiting a long time. Now, do we go forward or do you go home?"

I could see the look on his face was very serious. In that moment nothing would have stopped me from going forward with the ceremony. To be honest I never really thought about what I was getting myself into. I am not sure I cared. I felt like I owed it to myself and these people to know what I was actually there for. I just wasn't sure if I was ready for what I would find out.

"Yes I am ready." I was hoping I didn't sound to shaky. So typical of me to close my eyes and jump in at the deep end. Throw myself to the wolves, or jaguars, and just hope I come out the other side.

He smiled and motioned for me to come forward again. The crowd of people that stood before me parted slightly, taking a few steps backwards creating a corridor that I was supposed to walk through. I could see beyond them lay the temples on the hills, I assumed that was where we were going. Escorted by the gentleman on one side and the Jaguar on the other, we led a parade of people up the hills toward one small temple. It was hot and humid and I could feel myself starting to sweat. Every time we took a step forward, we created a tiny breeze, it felt so good in the oppressive heat. We climbed the small white steps to the top of the temple. I was very hot and each breath came only with extreme effort. As we approached the temple I could see a small door that led to somewhere. I could feel my fears starting to overwhelm me as I realized that door was there for me. The man in white walked over to the door, opened it and motioned as he said, "Now, get in there and sit."

"What do you mean get in there and sit? It is far too hot and I do not like small places. What kind of ceremony is this?" I was protesting because now, I was scared out of my wits.

"This is the ceremony as it has been practised for generations. Are you or are you not going to go in there and sit?" His voice seemed so much louder than before. So, I humbled myself and nodded slightly. I got down on all fours and crawled into the space. I shifted around to a sitting position just in time to see the door close behind me. I reached out to stop it, but it was already locked. There did not seem to be a handle on the inside. I sat there for a few moments trying to calm my panic and allow my eyes to adjust to the very dim lighting. The room was very small. I would not have been able to stand upright in it. It was long enough that I could have layed down but that was all. As my eyes adjusted to the light I could see right beside me was a very elaborate carving. It was a carving of a Jaguar. It was carved out of Jade and seemed to be luminous in the middle. The Jaguar was crouching and the mouth was open. Around the base there were many symbols carved into the block of Jade. I was wondering if it had been one giant block originally. It was beautiful and must have taken a very skilled person a long time to create. Jade is one of my favourite stones and I was most impressed to see something like this.

I am not sure how long I had been sitting there before I started to feel a lack of air. The room had heated up considerably since I had first entered. Breathing was becoming a little more difficult. Every breath took more energy than the last. I could feel panic coming up in me again. I was also starting to wonder what kind of ceremony this was, sticking me in a room with a stone statue.

More time went by and breathing was getting harder. I had not heard a sound coming from the outside. I was starting to question my sanity and thought I just need to wake up from this dream. I was so focused on my experience not being real that when I felt movement I reacted suddenly smashing my shoulder into the wall. I looked around quickly, thinking it must be a spider, and I don't like spiders.

but I could see nothing. I shook it off but stayed watchful. I had just started to settle back into my original spot and something brushed against me again. Again I jumped, but this time I thought I could see light in the statue's eyes. Just a flicker, just for a moment, no, maybe not. I must be seeing things. It was really hard to breathe now. My lungs seemed to be searching for every last bit of oxygen in the room. I was still trying to get myself to wake up when I could feel the energy of something pierce my skin. I opened my eyes and the Jaguar statue had come to life.

Its eyes were deep golden yellow and they were looking through me. Its body was still jade but I could see every muscle move. It was breathing on me, and I was terrified. I had to be hallucinating from the lack of oxygen. I reached out to touch it, and it screamed at me. I was not dreaming. I pulled my hand back slowly and stopped staring into its eyes. I put my head down in a gesture of respect and started to pray. I had no idea who I was praying to, but I was hoping someone would hear me. The Jaguar just stood there staring at me. It was panting and I started to realize that it seemed to be pumping air back into the room. I was breathing easier now, still scared but my lungs were no longer exhausted from effort.

Then the Jaguar spoke. "Why are you here?"

"I don't know. They told me to get into this room to finish a ceremony. So now I am here"

"NO! You have come for a reason. What is that reason? You must understand this now. If I stop breathing you will die. If you die here you will die there as well. What you are experiencing is real. Why do you continue to tell yourself you are dreaming? How do you know which life is the dream? Now tell me, why are you here?" His voice was commanding and it seemed to echo in a room that was too small to create an echo.

I was searching my mind for an answer to his demand, but nothing came.

"You are looking in the wrong place. What do your thoughts know of your heart. Your fears are getting in the way. What is fear? Tell me. What is fear? His voice shook the small stone room.

"Fear is being here with you!" I knew the second it was out of my mouth that it was the wrong thing to say. It was trying to be brave when that was the last thing I felt. It must have been a reaction to the shock of being in that situation. However I knew it was going to have ramifications.

"So you do not yet believe this is real". With that he reached out his paw and struck my on the side of the head. Instantly I could feel the throbbing start in my brain. It did the trick though, it woke me up. Now I knew it was real. I was there and so was he.

"Now answer me. What is fear?" I put my head down trying to control the heat and pain that was pulsing through my skin. "What was fear?" I didn't know. but I kept running it over and over. Fear was an illusion. Fear is what we feel when we don't feel like we are in control. Fear is what we hide behind when we are afraid of our own power. Fear is a state of uncontrolled negative anticipation. "Yes" That is it.

"Fear is what we create when we are not in control of a situation. Fear is being in a state of uncontrolled negative anticipation. Fear allows us to pretend we are someone different than we are. Fear creates the veil between illusion and reality." I knew that is what he was looking for. I think for the first time in my life, I understood what fear was.

"Are you afraid?" He asked in a low booming voice.

"No" My response was a whisper. In that moment I felt no fear. I cannot explain why, but there was no fear. In fact I felt nothing. I was in an extreme circumstance and I had no control. The only power I had was my honesty. So I let go, it was the only defence I had.

He looked at me, his eyes glowing yellow, "Ahhhh yes" was all he said.

I woke up in my bed with a raging headache and the feeling like I had been hit with a brick. I popped some Tylenol and tried to get back to sleep. Sleep was not to be had on that night. I lay instead and looked at a dark ceiling trying to make some kind of sense to the last few hours of my life. Making sense of anything did not happen either. As I could see the first streak of light starting to vibrate from behind the curtains, I closed my eyes and went to sleep.

I woke in a couple of hours because of two piercing eyes, hot breath and a wagging tail. My dog was trying so hard to will my eyes to open. It was past their breakfast time and he was standing as close to me as possible. His nose was almost touching my nose, but not quite, he was being polite. As soon as my eyes were open I was fair game. A few slobbery kisses later and I was up, out the door and walking in the morning dampness. The previous night was still weighing heavy on my mind. I didn't know what to think. I knew to get some answers I would have to go back. But going back meant, not knowing what might happen. Why was I so attracted to this place? It felt like I should be there, living there. I had this unexplainable ease around these people, even if they did lock me up in a tiny room with a Jade Jaguar. I was going back and I may as well not think about it anymore because it wasn't getting me anywhere. However that is not in my nature. I have to do things to death. So I continued to drive myself crazy with questions for the rest of the day. I should have been tired, but I never felt that way. Something unexplainable was happening to me, and all I could do is wait.

When I returned that night many people were standing around the large stone table. They were motioning and talking amongst themselves. I approached quietly and I didn't think they had noticed me.

"Approaching quietly? Is that from respect or fear?" And then they all broke out laughing. They were laughing so hard they could hardly contain themselves. I was confused at first, but that quickly morphed into anger as I realized they were laughing at me. They were laughing at my fear.

"What is wrong with you? Are you all insane? What gives you the right to laugh at me? You locked me up in a room where I thought I was going to die, with some freakish moving stone. How is that in any way OK? You are all completely fucked" I stood there shaking my head. I was raging inside. Completely disgusted. They were mocking my pain, and they had no right to.

Once they composed themselves enough to talk, they motioned for me to come and sit with them on the table. The coolness of the stone felt good against the prickly heat of anger that was coursing across the surface of my skin. Once we were settled I leaned back on my hands and waited for someone to speak.

"I am Teotihuan. I am the oldest one on your team. I am sorry for laughing at you. We forget that you have forgotten who you are. Let me tell you what you experienced in the temple and I am sure you will understand why we see it as something to laugh about. What you found in that temple was you. That statue is just a statue. It can only be activated by your emotion. That is why we heat the room and control the flow of air. It is like going on a vision quest but at high speed. We cannot tell you what you need to know. All we can do is set the stage for what you need to tell yourself. In your time there is a great deal of talk about belief systems. In that room your found out what you believe. You saw your own vulnerabilities manifest in an object and you projected authority into it. You gave the statue your power but kept your fear. You did this because you believe your fear is more real than your power. That is why the statue had to force you to see what fear was. Only then could you take back the power you had given away. You cannot feel two things at the same time. You made the choice to own your fear and be vulnerable to your power. Because you actually fear your power, you manifested a situation that had physical ramifications. You justified the reason to fear your power. This is what so many people in your time do. They fear their power and create a reality that justifies that fear. It is so much easier to own it. I am an old man, I do not have the energy to waste creating false realities any more. Do you understand you were the fear and you were the Jaguar, at any moment you could have stepped into that statue. But in your life you see your power as being something separate from you, so you manifest it externally as something that has control over you. Do you not see this?" He stopped speaking and waited for me to understand the point he was trying to make.

It took me a few minutes but I was starting to see what he meant. Because we fear our power, we disconnect from it. We separate ourselves from it, but that separation can never be truly complete. So we project it outside of ourselves where it takes the form of what we most fear. When we fear it we feed the fear. Because we have separated from it, we feel we are a victim to it. We create a reality of projected power over us, when in truth the power we are projecting is our own. If we could just choose to own that power, we would no longer have to project it in a negative way, and create lives where we can never figure out why we just can't get some things right.

What he was saying is that wherever we have a negative belief, we project it into the world to create a realty that usually causes us considerable discomfort. However in truth the reality we have created is just trying to get our attention about the power we are giving away. The discomfort is the gift, if we can accept the lesson. So what he is saying is that all the pain and suffering in our immediate reality is caused by our own projection of the rejection of our power. I had to take a minute and really think about this. This was a huge concept for me to grasp. I knew it was speaking directly to the circumstances in my life. This was my lesson, not just a general lesson. I sat there remembering as many circumstances as I could in my life, to see if this projection theory fit. After a dozen or so scenario's, I had to come to the conclusion, he was right. All I could do was shake my head and start to laugh. They were right, it was funny. All those things in our reality that we hated because they represented someone or something that had power over us, was just a reflection of the fear we had about owning our own power. We gave our power to the things we hated the most. Yes, that was funny. I found myself laughing hysterically, rolling around on the stone table. Why had I never seen that before?

"Now you see, we were not really laughing at you, we were laughing at the condition you think you live in. You are the masters of your own reality, you just don't want the responsibility. Come, lets walk the grounds and I will tell you more of this story and you will start to understand why you have come at this time. Initially we thought you had been prepared. Many that have come to us have gone through the initiation process and their memories have been returned to them. We did not initially understand you just sort of drifted in. However we are glad you are here and now we can tell you the stories of how you came to be here." The light danced in his eyes as he spoke. He may have been an old man but a child lived within him.

I was happy to spend some time with them now. I wanted to know the stories. I wanted to know why I was here. I knew now that no real danger was present here. I had for some reason chosen to be here. I could feel a new journey starting. Another new chapter in my life. Perhaps I would even discover why I have always had a magnetic pull to Mexico. Finally I was going to get some answers.

Chapter Two

As we wandered the grounds I could feel the sacredness of the land beneath my feet. Thousands of years of healing had happened here and it seeped into the earth. Every small breeze delivered a strong musky scent of the earth, mixed with a citrus scent from the trees. Life here was alive. I was so accustomed to 3rd dimensional reality and even in the wild places now, life was not so vibrant. Mother Earth had been badly damaged by people demanding more than they needed. To be in this energy where life was so present made my skin tingle. It felt like my cells were soaking in the extra oxygen and changing me physically.

We reached the end of the manicured field and turned to look back at the 3 small temples on the hill. I had such a sense of home here, and I could not explain it. I knew what each temple was and the meaning it had to the people. I knew that this area had served as a Spiritual retreat of sorts for those that ruled. I also knew that it was here that the Lemurian codes had been practised after being passed down through countless generations. I did not know a lot about the society that was referred to as the Toltecs but I had assumed this is where Teotihuan came from. I had to ask him to explain this to me as what I had been taught was different than the society I was experiencing.

"Yes the Toltecs. We are part of that society, yes. There were two types of priesthood in the Toltecs. The seen and the unseen. The stories you have heard about the Maya and the Inca and all the bloodletting, that was the Seen Priesthood. The Unseen Priesthood located our people in these little satellite communities. We practised the ancient sciences. The Priests that lived with the Royals and performed the sacrifices were there to put the fear into the people. The were crowd management. They had the false power that the people knew about. Most of them were power hungry themselves and would take an opportunity to marry into the royal line or even unseat one of the Kings. None of them knew of the cycles of humanity or the cycles of energy. Every year and sometimes more frequently than that the Royals would come here for healing and regeneration. We were however, kept hidden, if the other priests had known of us, they would have tried to dispose of us. We were written into history like a health spa. A place where the Royals came to be pampered. The other priests looked down on us like we were no more than glorified bath managers. This allowed us to do our work in peace. It was not often that a priest came here. When they did we acted appropriately. This is why you see no grand temples, nothing on the outside to bring attention to ourselves. However on the inside, it is a different story. The power here is held in the land. The land consciously participates in all work we do. The land teaches us and holds our memories as records. However to unlock the memories of the land you must first unlock the codes in your own DNA. Is this sufficient to answer your question?" he smiled a knowing smile as he turned his face towards the sun.

I was beginning to understand this man had no wasted movements, nothing was random here. Everything led to something else, and the only one that didn't know where it was going was me. I was trying to formulate my next question when Teotihuan said, "You wish to know why this place is so familiar to you?"

Yes, how did you know I was thinking that. "It is a very logical next step. You are connected to this place. You feel that connection and you wish to know what the connection is. Simple"

Simple for him maybe. I was still trying to get used to the lips not moving with the words. I found the only way I could do that was to not look at the lips. I had to focus intensely on his eyes if I were to not get distracted by it.

"Go wander over there, go behind that tree and when you come back towards the hill you will have the answer you seek." again said with a wry smile. So I did as I was told. There was a huge tree not far from us and I slowly wandered around behind it touching the bark. It felt like it was trying to say something to me. I wasn't watching where I was going and my foot banged up against one of the roots. I almost fell to the ground. As my attention was drawn down to my feet I could see I was no longer standing in the feet I woke up in that morning. I ran out from behind the tree looking at myself and trying not to curse.

I was wearing basic leather sandals, a long white tunic and a belt made of some kind of fibre. However more than that I was a man, a young man, with brown skin. I was have a difficult time walking because my centre of gravity seemed to be in a different place. My

14

body felt so flat, except for one spot. I quickly became obsessed with that one spot, it was so annoying, the only thing that seemed to rub against the fabric. I was not sure what to do, what had happened, or how to respond?

Then I heard the laughter. There they were all laughing at me and pointing once again. "Whats so funny, did you do this to me? Is this how I know this place?"

"Yes, this is who you once were. You were my student. You had promise. That was long ago now. You fell in love with a local girl and had a beautiful child. You did ascend to the 5th with your family and now you have returned to do it again. However this time you are there to teach, not to dilly dally. Do you understand?" His statement was lighthearted but his gaze was intense, I knew he was very serious about what he was saying, he just didn't want to bring the mood down. One thing these people loved to do was laugh. I was getting the idea that if I was to be around them, I was going to have to get used to their sense of humour and how I was most likely going to be the subject of it.

I still couldn't get beyond the body I was in, it felt so different than my female body. It was simpler, less attention grabbing. Practical was the way I would put it. My female body was complicated and it always felt like something was going on inside. This body felt a little vacant, rather boring, if I were to be truthful. Well that is all except for the bump in the front. If I was going to have to stay in this body I was going to have to get some duct tape to right things. An entire body and one little spot could be so distracting. I just could not focus.

"Go back behind the tree, it is clear we shall get no work done with you in that body." Teotihuan managed to express words in between the horrendous laughter. I circled back around behind the tree touching it as I went and then stubbed my foot again. Why can't I get this right? Oh, ok, good, ya, there are my running shoes again. Yep all is well again. I am lumpy and bumpy and saggy in all the right places. Ok I now have a new appreciation for how comfortable my skin suit fits me. Yes, better now.

"So that was really me?" Even though I knew it was me I still had to ask. I have done past life regressions, and during those moments you can see the experience you have lived, but I have never stepped into a former body before. I think I was still a tad bit in shock.

"Yes that was you. Your life here was lovely. You were happy and

15

you passed that joy on to everyone around you. You were very present in that lifetime. When you were working, you were working. When you were with your family, you were with your family. None of this all over the place as you do now. In some ways those days were simpler. We did not have people all over the world talking to us at all times of day. However we were charged with being experts at our chosen craft and the penalties that were paid if we did not achieve that excellence were usually paid in blood. Each time has its stresses and its joys. You just have to learn to navigate the space in between efficiently so you don't get stuck in either place." The wise one had known what I was thinking before it erupted from my lips.

"What am I here for now? I am really not sure I understand. I love it here but I am not sure how this fits into the life I am living now?" I was puzzled. I did not come looking for this place. I seemed to almost drift into it. But when I arrived they seemed to know I was coming. None of this experience really added up in my mind.

"I understand that all of this is confusing to you. The only reason it is confusing to you is that you did not expect it. It was not on your list. You have a soul contract to be here and to finish the apprenticeship you started with me. We are the Technicians of Light. We work with what you would call DNA. All things have some form of DNA. Even we have a form of coding. We are as human as you are, our frequency is just tuned to a different level. If you cut us we will bleed red as you do. If I were to go to your home, no one would know I was different. They may feel a difference coming from me but they would not be able to tell from looking at me. Correct?"

"Yes I think you are right about that. We would have to put you in some different clothes of course, but yes." I couldn't help but chuckle, thinking about introducing him to some of my friends. He would appear more different than he thought.

"So I have a job for you. If you wish to know what we do, it is best for you to have the experience. So next time you come here I would like you to bring someone with you. A friend, one of your clients or perhaps your dog. It doesn't matter who you bring as long as you have their permission and they are a willing participant. Ok with you?" And there is was, that smile that said, I know something you don't. This guy had a charm that could warm a bag of icicles.

"Ok, deal. I will do that. Then you are going to show me what you do?" I have a habit of feeding a question back to the person that asked it, just to make sure we are clear on our communication.

"Yes, you are correct. Now go home and sleep. You shall return in a few hours, and you don't need to be sleeping here." Off he went laughing again. I wasn't sure if the laugh was just because of his good nature or if there was something else behind it. I was curious now. Too curious to turn back. So off I went in anticipation of my return.

In a few hours I had returned with my dog. My beautiful boy was getting older and the climate we were living in did not suit him. Add to this, multiple injuries in his life and my suspicions around irresponsible breeding and you have a beautiful soul that feels less than beautiful. We were living in a maritime climate that had only a few frosts per year. As a result there were many bacteria and molds we were not used to. We had only been living here a short time when he started having breathing difficulties. All the vet could tell me was there was nothing wrong with him and she suspected allergies. To try and ease his distress I was using antihistamines and trying to keep him out of the worst areas. It was very stressful for him and very stressful for me. I was hoping the Technicians could help him.

As we walked across the lawn towards the huge stone table, some of the Technicians came walking towards me. They had not come to greet me, but they came to play with my dog. I had not seen any dogs in this community and they were very happy to have a furry friend to welcome. My dog took to them like he had known them all his life, which is very unusual, by nature he was suspicious and warmed to people rather slowly. Once they had their play time they placed my boy on the stone table. He laid down quietly and Teotihuan motioned for me to join him at his side. I was excited and nervous at the same time. I wanted to stay at my dog's side but I knew I would not be able to see enough from that vantage point.

I stood at Teotihuan's side and waited. One of his assistants placed what seemed to be a clear pink energy shell around my dog. He was showing no signs of anxiety so I was starting to relax as well. Once that had been done Teotihuan raised his arms and as he did, a visible energy field came up around the dog. In the energy field it looked like there were many different tiny holograms playing in a loop. I kind of squinted my eyes as though that would help me see better. I really couldn't believe I was seeing what I was seeing.

"Do you know what you are looking at?" Teotihuan questioned me.

"I am not sure. Logic tells me I am looking at his memories. It is like tiny little movies of specific things he remembers. But I am not

17

sure that is what it is. I only say that because some of those images I remember too, but I remember them differently?" I was held spell bound by what I was looking at. The harder I looked into the energy field the more I saw. I started to realize that many of the miniature movies I was looking at were only different because they were being viewed from a different angle through different eyes and different emotions. Somehow the movie was not only images but feelings as well. I didn't know how the feelings were being projected but I knew I could feel them. I could not explain to my brain, what my eyes were seeing.

"Beautiful isn't it? Some of the memories are painful yes, but to know your dog remembers all of this about you, and feels all of this about his life, it is a truth you were not expecting. What you are looking at is the recorded memory of his life, both with you and things he has done on his own when you were not present. The things you are looking at are the moments when he made decisions that somehow impacted and changed his life. Now let me adjust the filters. There I have taken away the happy moments, see how much less there is going on in the energy field now?"

I was having a hard time seeing, there were too many tears in my eyes. I wiped them away quickly and refocused. Yes, I could see it now. the moments that have caused him pain, even before I brought him home to live with me. I had no idea about some of those things. Others I knew all too well. "Yes, I can see it. I didn't know of this, how is it I can see all of this?" I wanted to know how to do this.

"All in good time. Now lets walk over there and we will be able to see not only the events that happened but how it is affecting him."

We walked over to my beautiful and patient boy who was laying there quite content. I gave him a pat on the head to which of course he nudged me into doing several times more. When I looked closely at the holograms I could see a filament of light linking the hologram to a specific spot on the body. This is where the event was anchored into the physical flesh and blood. If a problem was going to come from the event, it would start here. I could see in the holograms that the move to where we were living had taken up residence in the soft tissue of my boy's face, in his mouth and nasal passages. The move had just been so stressful for him, it had made him question his survival. How he eats and how he breathes had come into play. His fear was manifesting physically.

I had known before we left he was nervous. I did everything I could to make him comfortable and reassure him we would be fine. I could see now that he was just tired of moving. He felt his security was attached to his physical home. Every time we moved a little more of that security was chipped away. I felt so bad. I knew we were going to be moving again in the next few months. I did not know how to undo this damage. Guilt overcame me and the tears started to flow.

I went to my dog and apologized. I hugged him. I really did not know what to do to make it any better. I just wanted him to know that I loved him and I would try to make the next move the last. I asked him if there was any way I could make this moment better for him? Then someone tapped on my shoulder. I turned to see a finger pointing at an image in the hologram. The image that was anchored into the soft tissue was fading. It was not as bright as it had been and it seemed to contain slightly different images now. I didn't know what to think. I knew every decision we made had the potential to change the future but this decision was already in the past, how could it be changing now?

"Time is not constant, nor does it always flow in one direction. Time is very elastic and you can change it at will if you know how. The way your brain functions in your reality, time appears to flow forward. This is how you need to understand it to be able to link events together building momentum towards a goal. In your mind if you want to get to a goal there is a certain sequencing of events that need to happen in order to get to the outcome. If you do not follow those rules, you will not get to the right outcome. What if that were not true? What if you could affect your future by affecting your past? What if an apology undid damage and allowed healing to the extent that it eliminated the memory of the damage? If the memory of the damage was healed, then a negative becomes a positive and the imprint of an event can be released. Time as you have thought it to be, is in the process of changing in your reality. At least for those that know what time really is. This is how DNA can be affected through healing thoughts and emotions." Teotihuan walked away then, leaving me to think about what he had said. I was still in too emotional a state to really grasp what he was saying, but I know something anchored in me in that moment.

After a few very personal moments I walked back over to Teotihuan. I stood there quietly waiting for instructions. He looked at me with great empathy, understanding what my dogs meant to me.

My dogs were an extension of myself. What hurt them, hurt me. There was no separation between us. I did not see them as dogs. I experienced them as the beings that walk beside me. We were a pack, we took care of each other, we were a triangle of love.

"Now watch and learn. I will answer all of your questions after. Do not interrupt our work. There will be much that confuses you, but see if you can remember through the life you lived when you were here. It is still in your memories, try to access it."

Teotihuan walked over to the stone table and grabbed the hologram that had anchored itself in the soft tissue out of the energy field. He then stepped back a few feet and motioned what looked like a command to expand, with his arms. I could see what looked like the familiar image of a strand of DNA standing in front of him. The image was about eight feet tall and in full colour. I could see him scanning up and down the strand. He was looking for something specific. When he found it he reached into the image and removed a small chunk. He collapsed the image of the DNA and expanded the image of the small chunk in his hands. He kept expanding it and expanding it till there were beautiful columns of light in front of him. The columns of light stood in straight rows one behind another, eight rows deep. In the front row there was easily 100 columns of light. Each column was a different colour, but all colours seemed to be in within the spectrum of the rainbow. Some colours were more intense and some were pale. All of the columns were about the size of a fluorescent light tube, with very little variance. The second row seemed to mirror the first row with minor variations and so it was, through all eight rows. Each row a mirror of the one in front of it, with very slight differences. It was incredibly beautiful. Every light column was alive and pulsing. I thought I could hear sound coming from them but it was almost imperceptible to my ears. I could actually feel the sound more than I could hear it. It felt like a beautiful melody. Something that could carry you away into a dream.

Again Teotihuan was scanning the columns of light. He would gentle move them to one side and then push them back. I was mesmerized by the movement of the light. When he moved all the columns to the left a coloured fog seemed to follow behind. And the sound was like the most beautiful wind chimes you have ever heard, reacting in the distance to a slight breath of wind. It was hypnotizing. I found myself starting to sway to the movement of the light, and the subtle sounds they made. I was being powerfully drawn to the mystical dance of energy fluxing and flowing, pulsing through my being. I had forgotten for the moment where I was. This dance held my soul suspended within the universe and I could feel myself starting to drift away.

"Aha, here it is. There you go, I knew it was here somewhere!" Teotihuan:s exuberant declaration jolted me back to the present. In his hand he held one of the light columns that had gone dark. He passed the column to his assistant and then chose another column that was almost identical and put it into place. Then he collapsed the image back to a size that fit in the palm of his hand, expanded the image of the DNA strand and inserted the tiny piece back into its place. He collapsed the DNA image and replaced it back into the hologram. Then he walked over to my dog, gave him a big hug and said, "There you should feel better now." My dog gave him a big kiss and jumped off the stone table.

I stood there dumbfounded. I had no idea what had just happened. I could speculate of course, but it all seemed a little too surreal. I did think that it would make a spectacular scene in a movie. Teotihuan went to take a short break and I sat on the lawn soaking up the sun. My furry baby came running over to me and motioned that he wanted to go home. I had to respect that after everything I had just seen. So I announced that I had to go but I would be back as soon as I could for an explanation. Off we went landing softly in the world of dreams.

Chapter Three

As dawn emerged from the dark velvet skies, I lay in my bed still tying to understand what I had seen the night before. DNA as columns of light. I could understand how that was possible, because I believe everything is vibrating energy. Somehow seeing it in front of me, simplified to that level was what was tripping me up. I have read lots of things about DNA, only partially understanding what I was reading because of the terminology that was used, but I had never read about DNA as light. I have had personal suspicions about how DNA must interact with our souls, but knowing what is true and how the interaction occurs is another matter. I guess that is why I never became a scientist. For me knowing something to be true in my mind is often more interesting than having it proven to be true by another source.

There were a lot of questions running through my mind and wondering why I was involved in any of this was the front runner. I was not a healer and had no aspirations towards becoming one, so I was not sure why I had been privileged to see what I saw. I guess no matter how hard I tried to rationalize this, I was just going to have to wait until I saw them again to get the answers I needed. And that is only if they chose to give them to me then. I had been involved in many situations like this and when you are receiving information from unusual places they do not always answer your questions on demand. So I planned to return that evening again, and find something that would allow my brain to rest on the subject.

I emerged out of the mist and walked across the lawn towards the stone table. They were going about their lives in various ways across the land. I stood and just watched as these ancient yet future people lived their lives. If I was watching this scene on a documentary I would just think of it as normal people doing normal things, but the truth was far from that. I scanned the area for Teotihuan and he was not to be found. I wandered over to a young girl and asked for him, she pointed to one of the small temples that sat on the hill. The thought of going back in the temple was not one I cherished since my experience with the Jade Jaguar, but if I was going to get my answers

I was going to have to go places I would rather not. I opened the wooden door and it invited me into the darkness. As my eyes adjusted I could see Teotihuan sitting by a pool of water praying. I did not want to disturb him so I sat by the door and waited. He was chanting something I could not make out, but the rhythm was mesmerizing, hypnotic. I was just starting to drift when someone kicked my foot.

"You here to see me?" he asked with a big grin on his face.

"Yes please, if you have time." I was trying to scramble to my feet after being jolted back into my body.

"That is your problem, you cannot stay in one place. Everywhere you go you are somewhere else." He smacked his hand on my back as we walked past the wooden doors and into the bright sunlight.

We walked down the hill, across the lawn and back towards the stone table. Just beyond the stone table was a little hill covered in soft grass. This is where Teotihuan chose to sit. I took his cue and placed myself at a respectful distance from him. He sat there chewing on a piece of tree he had grabbed on the way over. He was waiting for me to speak. I was waiting for him to speak. I knew he could out wait me and I had no patience so I chose to speak first.

"Yesterday, what you did with my dog, that was amazing. I am most grateful, he is feeling better today. But I don't understand what it is you did to him. I don't understand what it is you are doing here? What am I doing here? What is this place? I know I am vomiting questions at you but I don't know how else to say what I need to say." Truth was, I was not even sure what it was that I needed to say. Oh it was all very clear before I got there, but when I opened my mouth to speak, gobbledy gook seemed to come out.

Teotihuan had heard every word I said. He sat there with that satisfied smile on his face. The same smile a cat has after it has just devoured a particularly tasty mouse. I knew he was waiting to speak, he was building the anticipation. He was wondering if I could keep quiet long enough to let him speak. He was a smart man and a good teacher, but I was anxious. My lesson now was to wait. So after a few moments of restlessly readjusting my position, I decided to play the game, I settled back into a spot in the grass and waited, and waited and waited. When I could wait no more I decided that maybe he just did not want to talk today. So I got up and decided to leave, I took three steps and he spoke.

"Where are you going? Do you not want answers?"

"I just figured maybe you didn't want to give me answer today and I do not want to waste anyone's time?" It was the truth, I could be getting some much needed sleep instead of being here for no reason.

"Are you present here now? I do not need you to be in two places at one time?" His eyes were doing that thing where he wasn't looking at me, he was scanning my energy.

"Well technically I am in two places, there is no way of getting around it." I said with some sarcasm

"I do not care about your body, it means little, you change it every few years. I am speaking to you, not your body. If you are present and willing to listen, we shall begin." I came back and sat back down in the same depression that I had already made in the grass. I was ready to listen.

"My people have been here for a long time. Our wisdom is not learned it is tradition. Each generation learns what is already known and adds to the knowing. If you are trying to learn something it means that you are going outside of yourself and looking to someone or something else for information you do not feel you have. Teaching someone never works unless that person is able to unlock the doors within themselves that lead to what is being remembered. In all of the universe there is no new knowledge, there is only remembering and returning. A good teacher has the ability to show the student where the knowledge lies within them. A bad teacher tries to own the knowledge and defeats the students spirit. Do you know how you come to understand what is taught to you? You must live it. Knowledge is alive. Our people are not taught, they live the life of knowledge from the moment they are born. We have no need for books, because the knowledge that you read about in a book, is lived each day here."

"Yes this is the 5th dimension as you have named it, but it is very little different from the vibration that you currently call home. Every morning when you get up and make a coffee do you have to learn how to do it? No, you do it automatically. Now think back to when you made your first coffee, did someone teach you? In your case no, you just decided to experiment till you found the taste you liked. Now over the years how you like your coffee has changed, no one has taught you to change your taste, it happened very naturally. As your personal vibration changes, your taste desires change, so it was all very subconscious. Can you remember the day you changed how you made your coffee? No, of course not. You were working from

25

that place of knowing inside of you. That is a place we all have. That is where the knowledge of the universe is stored. You think of it as your brain but it is not, the knowledge is stored in your soul and received by your DNA."

"You have a saying when you suddenly understand some information, you call it a "light bulb" moment. Well this is a very true statement. When there is need to understand something and the desire is strong enough, the light column in your DNA that holds that information is turned on, and the information filters down into your consciousness from there. However for that to happen the desire must be very strong and there must be a previous foundation of knowledge to build on. Instant knowing of chunks of information is possible but usually makes no sense when it happens with no previous preparation."

"My people live in a way that their daily lives involve use of this universal library. We have interacted with our DNA on a daily basis right back to Lemurian times. So if you are wondering if I can teach you how to do this, I would have to say no. However you can participate in the doing of it until you awaken the knowledge within yourself. Like I said though you must have a desire and you must have built a previous foundation of knowledge for this knowledge to make sense. Are you with me so far?"

Instantly I replied, "Yes", but as I leaned back on my elbows, I wondered if I did indeed understand. I would just have to keep listening and if he made a point that was truly beyond me, then I would ask a question, until then, I was happy to hear the story of this place.

"Good. Before we go on to talk more about the DNA, let me tell you about this world, what it is and how it is different from your existence. Our reality is not based on polarity. In your world you have the north and south poles and the earth spins on its axis. This represents how you as people can go to extremes either way in your life. Everything in your reality has an opposite side. If you are given a gift, only you can choose what that gift represents, it may be good, it may be bad, depending on the beliefs you have about the gift. In your world everything that you perceive is determined to be positive or negative based on your own personal experience of life. Choice is freedom, and for every choice you make there is both positive and negative about that choice."

"One of the biggest problems in your reality is that people get stuck in one way of perceiving. They can see everything as negative or everything as positive, and when that happens truth eludes them. Truth in your reality is based in polarity, the understanding that all things can be both good and bad at the same time, if the path of balance is not chosen. Would you say this is a good assessment of your world?" He looked at me waiting for an answer. I had assumed he was just going to continue. He already knew he was right, but perhaps he felt me drifting a little. There were times when the sound of his voice could lull me into that place between waking and sleeping.

"Yes, yes I think that is a more than fair assessment" I sort of coughed up, not wanting him to know I was listening to his voice like it was an echo.

"Alright, just wanted to make sure you were still with me." He laughed as he spoke. "In our world there are understandings that are absolute. Things are understood not so much as good or bad, but more as situations the evolve or dissolve us. We have circumstances here that you would see as being very bad or very painful, we see them as an event that is necessary for continuance in our evolution. Perhaps the best way to convey our understanding of our reality is there is no judgement about the circumstances or events in our reality. We see everything as an opportunity for evolution. This is the only way that we can maintain the necessary understanding that allows us to control our reality. You see this reality we exist in is consciously controlled by us. We understand that the wind is a reflection of our thoughts. All beings that grow and live here are a reflection of our feelings. The earth is a reflection of our reactions. The energy that ties all of this together is a reflection of our actions. We know our energy moves in five different directions, but I have only mentioned four to you haven't I?"

The sudden silence brought me back to the present moment. Teotihuan sat there looking at me waiting with raised eyebrows. I couldn't help myself, I broke out into laughter. The look on his face was so ridiculous. "Yes you have only told me of four. I am sorry but the look on your face was priceless. I was trying to visualize how the energy moves as you talk. I learn better if I can see what you say, so yes, sometimes there is a little delay in my response time, but don't think for a second that I am not hearing what you say." I knew he wanted an explanation even if he didn't say so.

"I see", he said nodding his head. "So as I am speaking you take the words in and go inside yourself and turn them into one of your movies?" Again with the raised eyebrows.

"Yes, that is what I do. For some reason this has always been my way of imprinting a conversation on my memory. Are you Ok with this?" I realized now that he may not like me doing this.

"How do you know you are seeing the things I say correctly?" His leathery face folded into new wrinkles as he cracked a smile.

"I guess I don't know for sure, I am just trusting that things are being translated properly."

"Well we shall find out later if you are seeing truth or not. The fifth way that energy moves is, it returns to you. What you put out into your environment, returns to you as your reality. In your world you choose to work with your energy in one of two ways. You internalize it and you become the problem and the solution or you project it so they out there are the problem, and something else is the solution. In this reality there are no problems and solutions there is only energy that flows to evolve or dissolve. You cannot project your problems onto another because the other does not exist. When you are consciously aware of the flow of your energy, you experience within yourself everywhere that your energy flows. When you have this experience, you feel inside as your reality feels outside. It eliminates the polarity, and creates unification. This is why only some people will be able to ascend to this place and maintain their reality. Here, reality is truly who you are. Here your reality can kill you, if you do not love yourself. Here if you project your pain onto something else it will project it back to you, undiluted. In this reality you learn who you are very quickly and make the appropriate adjustments or you perish. Now you may be thinking there is no such thing as free will here. It is the opposite that is true. Free will is the only rule we have here. You life is very literally in your hands."

"In our world there is no way to hide what you feel. Whatever you feel shows up very quickly in your environment. If you are sad, you may actually have rain fall upon you and only you. You may appear as though you are in a fog. You may temporarily not be able to move if your sadness is debilitating. However once you have processed the feeling you will return to your normal state. In your reality most people have a polarized opinion of emotional states. You think anger is bad when it is directed towards children, but it is justified when someone has offered you an injustice. Happiness is wonderful at a party but horrible at a funeral. Grief is something to be feared

28

because of the event that caused it. People in your reality do not experience what they feel, they judge the feeling and then avoid it or project it. It is not possible to do this in a 5th dimensional reality. Whatever is going on internally, will be on display externally. Are you understanding this?" He looked at me with compassion in his eyes. I could only imagine what he saw in my energy at that moment.

The truth was, I was rather terrified at the idea of everything I was, being completely displayed for everyone else to see. I considered myself to be fairly open with my emotions, but I was aware often of the rage or the suffering that I felt. It did frighten me of the damage I could do in a world that exploded my emotional reality onto a physical landscape, then fed that truth back to me personally. It was in that moment that I finally realized not only how powerful emotions are, but how powerful I could be. All these years I have either been swallowing what I feel down, or projecting it out there for others to have to deal with. I could appreciate the learning that would come from being a completely self contained emotional unit, but how would you deal with it. How do others deal with seeing what is going on in your reality but not being affected by it? My mind was starting to reel with questions based in fear. How would anyone be able to survive this reality?

"Remember what I said before, we are all one. What you feel and experience here, inevitably is felt and experienced by all. If your pain and suffering reaches a certain point, one of two things happens, you choose to perish or the world around you offers to absorb some of the pain and suffering for you. As I sit here beside you, I can feel your panic. I am choosing to allow you this experience because it is a healthy experience for you. Now I am going to absorb some of that panic for you. Do you feel the difference?" He looked directly into my eyes as he did something to me. I could feel a cool energy start in my stomach and release the fire that was consuming my organs, and yes it did make a huge difference. It was like someone just reached inside of me and took away the negative experience. I was amazed.

"Perhaps now you understand that sharing a problem is easing the problem. Here in this reality everyone feels your pain to some extent. If you were here you would feel the pain of others. It is in these times that we can choose to share the pain with them or not. Oneness is quite literal here. If you choose to share the pain, then everyone and everything feels better more at ease. In your reality most emotions are not shared because of the fear of judgement, however here nothing can be hidden. When nothing is hidden, people find ways to respect every individual life but still have separate lives. Now I know what I am saying may sound like a paradox but it isn't. It is through mutual feeling and mutual respect that we all experience each other as a community and as individuals. In your world and in my world we are who we are because of how we feel. Our feelings when expressed are released into the matrix to form a physical identity. However in your world you do not always see the manifestation that matches your feeling, there is a delay between what you feel and what you see. Here the delay is very short and we can easily connect what we feel to what we see. This is one of the biggest challenges to adapt to when you first arrive. I remember when we first came here. Everyone that arrived at that time were in a state of constant celebration. We had made it. We had left the oppressive old world behind. The energy of celebration that we pumped into the environment made this even more of a paradise. Everything we needed was at our finger tips. Over time, as is the way of things, old habits start to set in. You become relaxed and comfortable, and since everything was so available to us we did not think to consistently monitor ourselves. There were some that started to gossip, others got bored without the conflict from their previous lives, others yet, stepped into unwanted positions of leadership. It did not take long for our environment to change. And when it changed the people reacted to the change in a negative way. Our emotions had come alive and not all of us were prepared to deal with what we felt being projected back to us."

"There were species that appeared from nowhere. Species that are natural to this world but we had never before seen. Our energy had attracted them. Our world quickly fell out of balance and even the food started to get diseased and rot. We had teachers just as you will have teachers and they tried to show us what needed to change, but many could not handle the reality of their emotions being visibly expressed outside of themselves. They felt naked and vulnerable. We were not skilled enough to know how to absorb each others energy. So we started to judge and to blame and things just continued to get worse. Our teachers tried to get us to see, but we were blind. Most, simply could not handle seeing themselves. The more they saw the more they judged, and in the end most left this place. It was a very difficult time for us, and it is still painful to remember. If we had only known the true power of our emotions is not to tell another the truth, but to allow ourselves to experience the truth. The more we blamed another the less power we had to control our reality."

"I have told you time passes differently here. Five thousand years has passed in your reality since we left, only three hundred years has passed here. Can you see now, the difference in time delay that your emotions experience before they manifest?"

I had no idea what to say to this man. I had felt the pain he suffered trying to adapt to this place. It almost tore the heart out of me. I could understand what he meant about the time shift. I even saw some of the images he experienced and they terrified me. All the times I had been there and I had felt nothing but peace. I had just assumed that this was some sort of paradise, a gift from the universe for surviving the third dimension. I was truly having a hard time wrapping my mind around Teotihuan's truth. All I could do was sit and cry. There was no choice. I had to release the emotions I had absorbed from the images I experienced. I was releasing Teotihuan's pain. So I cried. I cried till I couldn't cry anymore. All the time the tears flowed from my eyes, I knew it was not my tears but I could still feel the pain. The pain was not mine but the tears still flowed. It was a very strange experience. I almost felt like I had volunteered to do this for someone else, and I was experiencing it all from a detached space. I was watching myself release someone else's pain. My logical mind could not comprehend it, so I stopped thinking about it. I was trying to let it flow through me without adding any of my own stress to it. Words simply are not enough to describe these feelings, and so I will let it be.

I needed a break now. It was a lot to deal with. I needed to think and understand what it was I was involved with. I still wasn't sure what I was doing there. I told Teotihuan I needed to sleep, and that was true. I also told him I just didn't know what to think about all this. It was confusing and almost felt threatening to me. He nodded as I spoke, I knew he would understand the challenge of what I was experiencing. He just made a small hand motion that said, "Off you go" and I did. I wanted to sleep but I also wanted space to try to make sense of this. I left not sure if I would return or not. All I remember from my sleep that night is feeling fear and chaos. I was happy to wake up even though I was still very tired. Normal had a new meaning for me in the moment.

Chapter Four

I decided that I needed to be in my familiar reality for a few days. I had a lot of work to do and I was super tired from all the learning I had been doing at night. I needed to do some sorting in my life. The real problem wasn't what I had experienced when I was there, the real problem was I now was more aware of what I was feeling and projecting. I was looking at my surroundings and apologizing after a bad day. I felt bad for my dogs when I was in a bad mood. I was stuck in the polarity he had been talking about. My experience had been one extreme and now I was stuck in the other. I needed to find the balance to stop my own suffering. So I started telling people around me what I had been experiencing. Not people in general of course, but specific people that I had a long standing relationship with. I found it did indeed ease my angst. I was also able to get some perspective on my experience. Sleep was still somewhat elusive as it was heavily saturated with elaborate dreams of Teotihuan's reality.

I was realizing just how unprepared I was for any transition that may happen. I could think of a lot of people that would not be ready for this as well. I had come a long way in dealing with my emotions but I was no master of them. I was hoping that when I returned to Teotihuan's reality, perhaps he could offer some kind of process or visualization to help prepare not only me but all the others that were ready to make the transition.

I lay down that evening with the intention of talking to Teotihuan about helping me prepare for this transition. I was tired and sleep came quickly. Soon I was standing on the expansive lawn looking towards the huge stone table on the left and the temples on the right. That sense of familiarity came over me again, as it always did. I was home.

I wasn't really sure where to go from here. I had had an experience where the world around me was not only alive but was physically participating in my emotional world. I was no longer an individual separate and responsible for my reality, I was an individual participating in the experience of a community reality. Everything I did affected the whole in a visible way. There was no where to hide. Adapting to living this way would be a challenge but I knew it could be done, I have seen the results. I was just hoping I could get some help. I would not be able to figure it out alone. So on this day I would find out what had to be done to help me change the relationship between my thoughts and my emotions.

Teotihuan and a few others were gathered by the stone table, they seemed to be discussing something of importance as I approached. I thought it always as bit of respect to ask if I could approach instead of just barging in on them. I was waved forward and I walked into the middle of a conversation.

"We are just discussing the best way to proceed with you, assuming you want to proceed?" He looked up at me, as did the others, I politely nodded my head. "Good, I think it would be best for you to see how the energy field interprets your emotions before we move on to actually working with the field itself. I think you should bring many people or animals to us that need healing. We will show you how to read the energy field based on what we find in it. Can you do this?" His mannerism was abrupt and straight forward.

"Yes I think so. I will just have to ask people if they want to go for a healing. So it is alright if I talk to people about you?" I had previously gotten the distinct idea they did not really want me discussing what happened there with others, so this request rather shocked me.

"It is fine to invite people for a healing, however to discuss exact procedures with them would not be a good idea. People are people and if they were to try and work with their own DNA without a safe guard they could do some damage unintentionally. Yes?"

He had a point. I was one of those people that liked jumping the gun and doing things on my own with very little training. Sometimes it worked out and sometimes it did not. No matter, he was right, DNA is nothing to mess with. So I agreed that I would find people to bring so they could show me how emotions build a reality within the energy field. From there they would teach me how the manifested emotions in the energy field projected themselves outward affecting or creating physical reality. It was not what I had in mind when I had come here this day but it seemed to make sense as a logical progression. So I thanked them for their time and their kind offer and I closed my eyes only to wake up in my bed. As I lay there, I was starting to think of ways that I might ask people if they want to go for a healing. It had never been part of the skill set I offered so I was not sure how it would all play out, but all I could do is try.

I put the word out as best I could and prepared to return to Bonampak that evening. I had learned that the physical region we call Bonampak in our reality was the same area that the Technicians of Light called home in the 5th dimension. Bonampak is a small temple area in Mexico, very close to the Guatemalan border. This is where the Technicians existed even when they were in the 3rd dimension, before they ascended. They have a long and illustrious history in that area.

I arrived on the grand lawn and walked towards Teotihuan who seemed to be waiting for me. When I stood in front of him he shrugged his shoulders as if to say, "Where are they?" Of course he was meaning that I was supposed to bring someone for a healing.

"I am sorry, no one has gotten back to me yet." I stated feeling kind of bad.

"You have a friend with a sick horse, Yes? We can work with him." He stood there nodding his head as he spoke, planting the word yes in my head.

"Yes, I think that would be Ok as long as the horse agrees."

"Ok, then, call the horse." He was matter of fact and rather dead pan in his delivery.

So I called Windsor's essence to ask if he would like a healing. Windsor was a majestic being. A beautiful horse that had helped many people heal their own emotional issues. He had collapsed a couple of times in the last week and being a senior gentleman his owner was extremely concerned about him. Windsor agreed to a healing and he got himself on the stone table. The Technicians covered him in a pink energy blanket and they set about working on him. They stood back and focused on him momentarily and as they did this, his energy field became visible. It was clear that fluids were not circulating properly. There seemed to be many spots of flow that were dammed up. There was also a disturbance that was hard to describe. Almost as if the energy field was not clear, but instead was covered in static. As I got close to the projected image of Windsor's field I could see the static looked like many many tiny little worms all squiggling about in every direction. The image made me feel all creepy crawly and I started to scratch.

The Technician's now had a direction to work in. They started moving the fluid and simultaneously working on the area's that were dammed up till each spot was opened and the fluid energy was flowing properly. Then they massaged all the fluid to Windsor's hind quarters so it could be eliminated. Next they inserted what looked like a stint and started pumping green energy into his heart, which in turn pumped through his body. I was told they were doing this to build his blood and to raise his vibration. As this green energy pumped through his body and was evacuated from the rear, you could see him starting to stand taller and vibrate with energy. The Technicians said that the loss of energy was from the parasites, who love to feed on highly evolved beings. They told me that parasites are trying to evolve as well and they will always seek the highest vibration they can find.

This fascinated me because I know many spiritual people that are plagued with worms and don't think they should be. In fact I know many people who don't think humans get worms the same way animals do. That was a piece of information I would stash away with the intent to do my own parasite cleanse.

At a certain point Windsor's energy field seemed to spontaneously clear. There were a few things floating around that the Technicians removed because they were no longer serving his purpose and then it was over. I was assured that he would be fine and that his caretakers were taking care of the physical being in a way that would make this so.

Windsor seemed happy and was kicking up his heels so I said good bye to him and off he went back to his physical body. I was happy he seemed to feel better but for me the proof would be when I talked to his owner the next day and found that he was indeed feeling much better. And yes there were physical actions taken that healed what the Technicians had pointed out to me. I was now becoming a believer in what I saw in the energy field. I still did not know how they brought the images up to look like I was watching a super sized hologram, but it was fascinating and I wanted to learn more.

"What a beautiful being. He is old, very old. He probably knows more than all of us combined. I could feel his energy tracking back to the beginning of time. I was honoured he let us work with him." Teotihuan stood there feeling satisfied. His energy was calm and grounded. He sat on the lawn and said a silent prayer, then he pulled a tiny bit of grass from its roots, blew on it and made an expansive motion with his hands. He gently patted the ground beside him, motioning for me to sit and I obeyed.

"Do you know what you saw?" Teotihuan looked deeply into my eyes so he could see the truth of what I was about to say.

"Hmmm, Yes and No. I could clearly see how Windsor's fluid flow was dammed up, however I did not know what all the little squigglies were. I actually thought it might be my eyes trying to adjust. However I do know looking at those things made me scratch. What was that green stuff you were pumping through him?" I knew I understood the process of what they were doing but I had no idea of the substances.

Teotihuan smiled then he spoke, "That was the energy of the heart of plants. In your reality you understand that plants are sentient beings, however you also understand they are not sentient in the same way humans are. A species of plant is more like a single unified cell. When all the species of plants come together they make a body. Each individual species communicates with other species to make their environment a harmonious one. Plants like human express their emotions in a physical way, however humans usually turn it into some kind of grand gesture. Plants literally inject their emotion into their environment. Through releasing scent or sudden growth. In some cases they will change their own chemistry to expand or contract their physical presence. When a plant is having an emotional experience you will feel it or see it, you will become part of the experience although because you don't speak plant, you may not know this is what is happening. When we inject depleted beings with the heart of plants what we are doing is sending them the energy that is found in the heart of the plant people. Basically we ask the plants to love this being in such a way that the nutrient that represents plant love fills the veins. Doing this is one of the eight processes of longevity. It works like a tonic and revitalizes. People in your reality understand the value of absorbing nutrients from physical substances. If you do not have the right balance of vitamins and minerals you will die. Here we need the same nutrient balance, but we choose to absorb our nutrients in a way that will not rob the source of its life. We ask for a donation of love or energy. Sometimes we ask for a donation that will enable us to think better or remember more. When we need something we turn to the masters of it. The masters of all we need, live in the world around us. Does that help you to understand?"

I thought about it for a moment and yes it did indeed help me to understand. Still though I did not understand how the energy got from the plants to the person that was receiving it. "Yes, thank you. How do the plants give you their essence if you do not put it in your mouth and chew?"

"It is hard for you to let go of what your have spent a whole life learning. You may think that energy comes to you through ingestion followed by digestion, however as you body becomes lighter and lighter there are many practices you will no longer be able to tolerate. Eating will be on that list to a certain extent. Do we eat? Yes but we limit ourselves to the things that raise our vibration. This dimension is about conscious evolution. So the rules you work within here are all focused on that goal. It would not serve that goal to eat food that caused you to devolve. You still have free will here but the choices you have are much more limited. If you come here and decide to stay, you will no longer want to abuse yourself. You will come to serve self love as a master, because truly loving yourself is the only way you can truly love another to discover Oneness. Is this what you were asking?" Teotihuan lay back on the lawn knowing very well I had a million questions and would not ask them. I needed to sort this out for myself and then decide what was important enough to ask.

"I will sit with this, if that is alright with you? How can I learn some of this stuff for myself? I have seen much and I am coming to understand the basics but can you give me something to do that would increase what I see?" I was really feeling the need for this. Some practice I could do in my waking life that would allow me to see more of a 5th dimensional reality, or at least expand what I already knew.

Teotihuan sat very still. I could almost see the wheels turning. I am not sure he was expecting me to ask this question so soon. It took a few minutes but he turned to me looking very pleased and said, "So you want to become more? Alright. I will give you a process and you can practice it at home. I will not tell you what it does. I want you to tell me what it does after you have worked with it a few times. Does this work for you?"

"Sure, that would be great. I look forward to this." I was very excited and waited for him to describe the first process to me.

Find yourself in a place that is comfortable and quiet. Allow your body to be completely supported by what is beneath you. Breathe deeply. Let you mind relax. Close your eyes and breathe deeply. Relax all your muscles one by one starting with your feet. Relax everything even your scalp and your hair. Now when you are very relaxed I want you to imagine you are in a beautiful bathtub. You have just sunken down into perfectly warmed water. Put some salt in the water so it makes your body feel even more weightless. As you lay back in the tub you can feel the heat moving from your skin into your muscles. The gentle warmth moves deeper and deeper into your body. It cleans and it heals as it goes deeper internally. Soon you are feeling the warmth in the very centre of you body and you are so relaxed you don't want to move. Your body is so comfortable you cannot feel it, all you feel is the warmth and the safety of the salty water.

Now let your mind drift. Let it drift to a place when you were very happy. A moment in time when all that existed was joy. You can feel the happiness spreading throughout your body. It spreads from the centre outwards to your skin. The joy then continues to move outward, moving joyously through your skin and into the water. Allow your joy to tint the water a certain colour. As you do this you can see all the water slowly turning the colour of your joy. You are now floating effortlessly in a tub of warm coloured water. Can you see what colour your joy is? How does the colour feel on your skin? Does the colour have a message for you? Allow the message to gently filter into your thoughts.

Now allow the warm salty water to fully support you in the beautiful tub. Close your eyes and ask your body to allow an image of your joy into your energy field. Feel this image gently form and rise a few inches above your body. Now with your eyes still closed count backwards from 10 to 1. See each number clearly as you count backwards. 10, 9, 8, 7, 6, 5, 4, 3, 2, 1 and then gently open your minds eye. Right in front of you, in your energy field you can see a little hologram of the image of your joy. What is that image? Where is it located on your body? Are there people in the image? If so, who are they? What are you doing in the image? Try to get as much information as you can from the image. When you have as much information as you can get, reach out and hold the image in your hands. Pull the image close to you. Is there anything else you can see now? When you have everything from the image you need, take the image and place it in your heart. Know that this image will gently dissolve within you and send all of its joyous energy through your body.

Now find a spot on your body that needs healing. Allow the colour that is in the water to be drawn towards the spot that needs to heal. Watch as the colour slowly gently moves through the water and into the spot on your body that needs healing. As the warm salty water starts to return to its clear nature you can feel the colour working its magic and spreading throughout your whole body, healing all spots with its joy. Your body is warm and relaxed. You feel whole and complete. Now once again count from 1-10 and when you are ready open your physical eyes and choose to not move too quickly for a few minutes.

"Thank you. I will work with this over the next few days and hopefully understand what it does for me." With that I got up from the lawn and walked back into my 3rd dimensional reality. For many more nights I would take many volunteers to the Technicians for healing. Each one was different and fascinating. I came to see that there is no such thing as a standard healing. Everyone's energy field told their story in different ways. Some people had many past lives in their field and healing those was their focus in this life. Others had physical ailments. The physical ailments could easily be repaired with a DNA manipulation however the emotional habit that caused the problem was more difficult to change. I watched and I learned. I came to see that healing is always multi layered especially for people. For animals most often it was straight forward. Find the problem fix the problem. There were a few animals who were carrying illness for their owners and the only way for them to heal was to get the owners to heal. These were the most difficult cases. The animal was a willing participant, but how do you tell the owner that if they don't change their ways, their beloved pet will die. The owner either becomes riddled with guilt or enraged with anger at such an accusation. I have never found an easy way to deal with this situation and probably won't. Until pet owners come to understand the extent they are intertwined with their fur family, they will have a hard time understanding sudden illness or the guilt that follows.

This is not only true for pet owners. We are all inextricably intertwined with our reality. Everything we do, think and feel affects something or someone else. It is time for us to open our hearts and open our eyes to see who and what we are attached to. In this way, by choosing to heal ourselves we can help heal all those we are attached to. Initially it may feel insurmountable but inevitably it is unavoidable.

Over the next weeks I worked with the above process. I was always intrigued at how the colour in the water always seemed to be the colour I needed to heal my aches and pains. I used this process not only to explore my joy but to understand my fear and illusions. I found that this process could be adapted to most parts of my life that were in question. If there was something that I needed to see to help me explain how I had become who I was, this was the process I used to help me discover that.

Chapter Five

I was still very curious about the 5th dimension and how it differs from the world I lived in. I wanted to know more. I was not sure how much Teotihuan would tell me but it would not stop me from asking. I had grown very comfortable with him in the past months. I really enjoyed the time I spent in Bonampak. He had told me that 5000 years ago this small temple area was where they had been located. About 100 years before the ascension was to happen, everything started to speed up. This is what Teotihuan told me, "Peoples all over the world became needy and dependent on the words of the leaders to run their own lives. They had uncovered large amounts of information about the Atlantean times and all people regardless of training were trying to work with alchemical magic. People became obsessed with power and becoming part of the Royal house. At the very least they would not rest until they had others that slaved for them. But worst of all, the people became arrogant. They deemed themselves the greatest thinkers, the greatest craftsman and the greatest leaders that had ever lived and they did whatever was necessary to make themselves believe it. While those with power took power from others, they also grew paranoid with fear of having power taken from them. The use of powerful and addictive substances allowed Kings to think they were gods. Most of those in the Royal house were under the influence of something all the time. Once they had dreamed of their own glory, they did not want to experience who they truly were within society. This led to much of the bloodletting. Minds became distorted and twisted, the fear of having to be who they were was projected onto the people. Their thirst for blood did not end with sacrifice. It spread like a sickness in the sacrificing of lives in the mines as well. Precious stones became a status symbol. Lives where traded for things that sparkled.

Time was compressing in preparation for the shedding of Earth's 5th dimensional skin. Many minds could not take the pressure they felt inside their head. It drove some crazy and it drove others to suicide. As the shift came closer we could start to hear the people that were in the 5th dimension we could hear them on quiet nights, we could hear them in our minds. Sometimes when we were alone we would see them, like we were looking through a mist, and they could see us. Very few of us knew about this shift. To speak of it was blasphemy and the sentence was death. Those that were in power did not want the people to think there was a saviour just beyond the veil. We knew of the shedding of Earth's skin and did all we could to prepare ourselves and our people. However it was not enough. Without having direct access to our people, there was only so much we could do to prepare their energy. We had to wait till the shift was over and hope that we could teach them quickly enough to stabilize them in the 5th.

This did not happen as you know. Only a small portion of us came through. It was a very difficult time for our people and for our hearts. But this is the way of Earth, every 5000 years, she sheds her skin. For those that stay on the old Earth, the people that ascend become the legends and stories for coming generations. The shedding of the skin causes much unrest and upheaval, but it is a natural process. Time speeds up and much heat is created by the friction of the skin releasing from the mother. The grid system that holds the memory of Earth shifts and the beings that incarnate on her afterwards have a different experience than those that came before the shift. Earth has an infinite number of incarnate experiences available. Each time the grid shifts it is like turning a knob to a slightly different reality. In this way, you can incarnate on Earth many times in many different realities and learn the same lesson in many different ways. Like a person changes their clothes, Earth changes her experience. This is how Earth evolves."

I had heard him talk about this a few times and I still had a difficult time swallowing it. Most of us on Earth at this time have grown up with the traditional Creation or Evolution theories. This did not really fit into either one. However if I took into consideration legends and folklore, it did explain a lot. Specific memories were in play when the grid system was anchored in specific spots. Earth's memories were a plethora of 5000 year time sequenced dramas, designed as a back drop for the beings that came here to play out their incarnations and learn their lessons. Hard for me to fathom but made complete sense.

The extremes that had happened in Teotihuan's world just before the shift, were happening in mine. Same thing, different methods.

Time was speeding up exponentially. This only made sense due to the fact that we had to catch up to the speed of time in the 5th. There had to be a meeting point of the two worlds for Earth to be able to shed her skin before the tremendous release from the old Earth where time would then slow down to a stand still. It was easier when I thought of time as Earth's pulse. With the tremendous amount of energy she was expending preparing to shed, her pulse was quickening to the point of passing out. Only to return to a resting rate once she let go and chose to rest.

"Metaphor's are a wonderful thing aren't they. They allow us to understand complex idea's we normally wouldn't, and that makes us look smarter". He laughed as he came up to me. I hadn't even noticed his approach, I was so deep in my own thoughts. This was the first time I had been involved with beings that were still human but in a place of higher understanding. I honestly had not adjusted to the constant sense of humour yet. I was accustomed to beings that I considered lofty or unemotional, usually extremely wise, but definitely not human.

"You startled me! I was deep in thought, thinking about some of the things you told me about this place."

"Hmmm, you keep calling it this place. Is it so difficult for you to think of it as Earth?" Teotihuan rested his back against the great stone table, folded his arms across his chest and rested his chin on his fist. He had a very playful look in his eyes, it made me nervous.

"I guess I am just not really comfortable here yet. It is so beautiful and appears to be so perfect but I know that is not possible. No place is perfect. I have been to Mexico in my reality and I love it there. It is beautiful. This place looks just like it. However you and your people look like you are from a time 5000 years ago. In a way this all seems like a movie set to me. How is it you know so much about my world and what it is like when you were never there? You left my Earth 5000 years ago, but you know what computers are and nanotechnology. You seem to know more about my world than I do? Honestly, it is a little disturbing when you can tell me more about my reality than I can, and you always seem to be right. That is a little hard to adjust to, when you claim to be just human." I realized I was sounding a little accusatory towards the end, but it was nagging at me. They say they are human then why aren't they human like me?

"Ah yes, why aren't we human like you? There it is. There is the thought that will prevent you from being human like us. That is the thought that keeps you attached to the type of human you are. You consider yourself a very open minded person, and comparatively so it is true. However no matter how open minded you may be, you still have your attachments to your identity. This is not always a bad thing. Having an attachment to your identity allows you to be who you are, and recognize the face you see in the mirror everyday. It helps you keep your identity intact. That is truly necessary for you to function in any reality. However when you become so attached to your identity that you are wanting other people or beings to be like you, well that is a symptom of attachment debilitation. You identify so strongly with your own reality that accepting that we are human, albeit a different kind of human is borderline unacceptable for you. So tell me now, what is really bothering you about us?"

I could tell Teotihuan was softening his energy, trying to engage me, lure me in so I would let him in as well. And now I knew what that playful look was in his eyes. He had led me like a fly to his web.

I stood there for a moment contorting my face into many shapes as though I could avoid the question with expression. Pursing my lips thinking I was about to say something and then nothing would come out. Teotihuan stood patiently, softly looking at me. Then finally I just sort of blurted it out, "I think I am afraid I might not make this transition. There is no evidence this shift is even real? When it comes down to it, I just don't know what to think, and I am scared. You always seem to be so calm and know exactly what to do. I can't compete with that!"

"Good, now the elephant is stepping on the toes of the people." he just stood there smiling again.

"Don't you mean the elephant in the room has been revealed?" I said politely

"Yes that is the expression from your reality, however in this moment I think the elephant is stepping on our toes".

I felt bad. I felt like I had insulted them and all they have done to teach me. I became wracked with guilt and wanted to run back home. So I started to apologize, fearing I had destroyed my chance to learn from these people. I guess the very fact that I had insulted them should tell me they were human after all.

Teotihuan couldn't hold on any longer, he burst out into laughter so intense he dropped to his knees and started rolling on the ground. Pointing at me and laughing, why were they always doing this? Now I was so frustrated and embarrassed I wanted to turn and leave. Ok, now I knew these people were definitely human. Baiting me to bare my soul, then making me feel bad for baring it and finally laughing at me for being so stupid as to bare it. I threw my hands up in desperation and started to walk away.

Teotihuan came running after me and grabbed my arm. I shot him a look that made him literally step back a few feet, he doubled over in pain. I freaked out. Now what had I done. As soon as I released the rage from my gaze he recovered. I ran to him to make sure he was Ok. He stood up straight gasping for air as he did and said, "Now, do you have a better understanding of what this place is all about?"

We returned to the stone table where he allowed it to support his weight for a few minutes as he recovered to full strength. He then continued with his explanation. "Until these last few minutes we have not allowed you to participate in our reality. You have been an observer only. You energy was blocked diverted as need be. You have been quite stable at all times when you were here. So it was time to see what you could do once we removed the block on your energy. Before now you had not formed an attachment to us, so poking the tiger would not have worked with you. I could only cause a reaction in you if you cared about me. It is nice to know you care so deeply it hurt. This morning when you knew you would be coming we drew straws to see who would bare your wrath, I lost." Teotihuan was still laughing as his energy returned to normal.

Ok so I had been set up, cause they wanted to see who I really was or what I was capable of. I still felt quite betrayed. I suppose he was right though, the only way to get a pure reaction, was to ambush me. Smart really, but still annoying.

"Look around you. Look at the plants. You have been focused on me and not your surroundings, so look now."

I did take that moment to look. Everywhere I had stood when I was having an intense emotional reaction, the plant life was in a state of returning to normal The grass under my feet had formed a swirly pattern trying to get away from me. Some of the plants on the edge of the forest had pulled their leaves back towards themselves to avoid the blast of rage energy that came from me, and were just now allowing their leaves to spread again. I walked over to a tree that was close to me and much of its bark had been disturbed. It looked like someone had taken a giant cheese grater to it over a three foot section. I apologized to the tree. I apologized to the grass and to the plants. I stood and raised my hands to the sky, spinning slowly sending love in every direction, it was all I could think of to do. And in a few minutes all seemed right again, although the tree would continue to bear my scar.

"Once again, do you understand how this world works now?" Teotihuan spoke with absolute compassion in his voice.

I lowered my head and nodded slowly. Emotion was a physical thing here. It had great power. If it was not consciously focused it could easily destroy.

"You are strong. You have great passion. Though it may not be as apparent, this same energy occurs in your world as well. In your reality you have filters that allow you to shield yourself from the physical impact of emotional energy. Since you are so attached to your thoughts, the emotional energy gets drawn to your thoughts like a magnet. So you end up misrepresenting thoughts for feelings. This attachment is so deep that words make you feel whatever emotion you have attached to that word for your entire life. Much of this will occur in your young life when you are having an intense experience and hearing words that are being said during that experience. In many cases the words you hear may have nothing to do with the experience you are having, but you link them irregardless. Now, the real difference in our humanities is that we do not feel through our words. We are very aware that they are two different experiences. One is used to convey how we think the other is used to convey who we are. Do you understand the difference between the two?"

I really had to stop and ponder this. Emotion reveals who we are and words reveal how we think? I did completely understand the concept however I was not at all sure I could sever the two.

"I can see you are a little perplexed, so let me help you. In your reality because you are not conscious of the separation between these two things, you think that what you say and what you do are coming from the same place, this is not true. The action you take in life will always come from who you truly are. What you say in life will come from who you perceive yourself to be. Does that help?" Teotihuan really wanted me to get this right. He was leading me to the water and waiting for me to drink.

"So you are saying I am some kind of a major bitch because of what I did to you and not the nice person I think I am?" Even though there may have been some truth in that, I was still a little miffed.

"No, now you are taking my teaching our of context because you think I am attacking your character. The truth behind the statement you just made is that you are afraid you will not be accepted by us and that affects your self worth. So you take my words and attach your emotion to them. Now do you see what I am trying to convey?"

"Yes I think I do. You are saying that a great fallacy in our world is the assumption that our words speak a truth about our emotions. Are you also saying that words spoken with no emotion attached have very little power?"

Teotihuan smiled a huge toothy grin at me. I knew I had done something right. He nodded and started to speak, "Yes, that is right. When people you have no attachment to, say something that displeases you, you don't really care. However if someone you loved very much said something you thought was hurtful you would despair. It is not the words that have bothered you, it is the emotion you attach to the words. Now here is the point that brings chaos to your world. Not all people attach the same emotions to the same words. You know this. This is where communication breaks down and breaks apart. In our world words and emotions are two different things. We can choose to consciously attach emotion to words if we want to. We often do, especially when we speak to our children or to our partners. It is a lovely thing to do and to experience. However linking the two in an inextricable way can be very detrimental. To function in this reality you must learn to separate the mind and the heart. Here the throat and the heart chakras are merged. So to not have control over your words can lead to your demise."

I let that sink in. I knew he was right. It made perfect sense but it seemed to be an overwhelming task. How can you unravel an entire lifetime's worth of emotional word attachments? If I was going to learn how to do this I would have to have some kind of interactive experience, and not someone poking the tiger. I needed to be able to take a look at what emotions I attached to what words. So I asked Teotihuan to create a process for me. I needed it to be something that I could do in my own reality in my own time. A private practicing of sorts.

He agreed it would be a good thing for me to understand in a more personal way. He said next time I came there he would give me something I could experience in a visual way that would help. I was feeling very tired now and just wanted to rest, so I said my good byes and left for the comfort of my bed.

I returned again in a few days. I always needed a bit of a break when things had gotten intense. Teotihuan welcomed me with a warm smile, he seemed pleased with himself as he started to describe this next process he had designed.

The first thing I want you to do is decide on two words that you would consider to be highly emotional words. Choose 1 positive and 1 negative word. Next I want you to find a comfortable place to be where you won't be disturbed by anything outside of yourself. Settle yourself into a place where you can become totally relaxed. Allow whatever is below you to fully support your body. Breathe deeply and slowly several times to find your centre. Once you feel clear, I want you to close your eyes and imagine you are in a truly magical place. This can be any place that makes you feel like you are limitless. The environment around you loves you and acknowledges your very presence. There may be trees and lakes or maybe you are in a beautiful castle. Choose a place that has magic for you. Allow yourself to be fully present in this space.

Now, interact with the environment around you and it will respond to you. In this space you feel loved by everything, this is your world with no one else to influence it. You are comfortable and relaxed, this space opens it arms to you. You smile and the world around you smiles back.

Slowly now, allow yourself to think of the negative word you chose. Allow it to slowly enter your consciousness. Let yourself feel the word and all the emotions you have attached to it. Go deeper and deeper into the word till the emotion of the word seems to become a physical thing. Allow that emotion to amplify inside of you till you think it is going to explode out of you, then at the last second yell the word into your environment. If you feel safe to do so, you can yell with your voice, if not you can yell in your mind. Make sure you explode every bit of emotional energy out of you in the expression of the word. Your body should feel like you just had a huge release, tired but good. Now slowly without moving your body, use your eyes to explore the direction you yelled in. Look closely at whatever is in front of you. Is there any difference from what was there before? Is there damage? Is anything distorted? Is there a feeling of pain coming from that direction? Use all your senses now to feel what that area felt when you yelled at it. Can you sense what it felt? Is it communicating with you in any way?

Now look deeply into that same area in front of you. Ask yourself why is this word so emotionally charged for me? Focus on wanting to know what event in your life caused you to attach those emotions to that word. Keep looking forward and you will see a mist starting to appear. As the mist grows bigger, you will see an image appear from your past. It may be a snapshot, or it may play like a movie. You may hear words or have strong feelings. Look deeply into the image and remember what was happening in your life at this moment. What you experience now will answer why those emotions are attached to that word. Allow yourself to fully experience this. As long as it is safe, bring it into your body. Remember what you felt. Remember what you heard. Now if you want to change the emotions that are attached to this word, allow yourself to rewrite the scene. Change the scene to what you need it to be so you can attach a different understanding to the word. Once you have rewritten the scene I want you to say the word and attach the new meaning to it, like this, _____ makes me feel _____
Insert the word followed by the emotion you want to feel, then replay the rewritten scene in your mind.

You have now anchored a new emotion to an old word. Now go back to the beginning and rerun the process with your positive word. Take note of how different everything is with the positive emotions anchored to the positive word. Allow yourself to fully experience this difference.

"You can use this for all words that are emotionally charged. You can also use this to separate words from the emotions you have attached to them. Now please do not get the wrong idea, attaching emotion to words is not a bad thing. However to be truly effective, the emotion that is attached to a word must be attached in a conscious and controlled way. Whether it be in your time or mine, this is how all great leaders lead, they provoke emotion in their audience with carefully crafted emotionally attached words. However if they are not in control of the emotion they are working with, often they are considered lunatics instead of visionaries. Now go home and play with this process, you will find it very effective and very interesting, to see how words have crafted your emotional life."

With that he turned away in a completely unemotional manner and wandered off. I went back home to see what personal history I could speak into being.

Chapter Six

Things were progressing very nicely towards an educated transition. I felt like I was starting to understand at least some of what I was being taught by the Technicians. I really liked their teaching style because they would only ever take me so far and then they would demand that I worked with the processes or took a break from them. They always knew before I did that I was getting a little exhausted.

During my little break I indulged myself in a favourite pass time, mind bending movies. I have always been very partial to fantasy movies that feature hero and heroines with special powers. Over my life's span I have seen many, and each in turn has stuck with me for one reason or another. I am not a fan of violence, I like a movie that's uplifting and brings hope. I do admit that my delight in such movies has been lessened over recent years because some of the CGI work is just getting too overdone. So finding that movie that is just right is a challenge.

Over a few days I found a variety of movies that normally would delight me. However I would watch a portion of one and become very quickly bored. I was really disappointed by this. So I sat and thought, trying to examine why this was happening. Was I just getting old? Did I have no imagination anymore? Then it came to light that I was no longer looking for powers. I know in the past I thought it would be great to be able to magically affect your surroundings. Wave a finger and save a world, kind of stuff. But that just wasn't doing it for me now. As I examined this new awareness it came to my understanding that I was no longer interested in powers because my self identity had changed. Yes it is true that to have powers would allow you to be of great benefit in helping humanity if used wisely. However I was now seeing that to have powers was to make humanity dependent on one person. Having powers was either a blessing or a curse and sometimes both, but it did very little to help the individual find their own power.

I had gone from wanting powers to understanding how powers are more of a by product of true authenticity. Powers are inevitably a trap in and of themselves that allows the rest of the world to label you as this or that. In most cases the hero in the movie with the powers is celebrated in the end, but that is only a movie. In reality the hero with the powers is most likely consumed by his own ego or feeling enslaved to a public. Powers do not empower the people. They lure the people into a false sense of security.

I no longer wanted powers. I wanted something that would help empower the people, and that is why I am just not that attracted to fantasy movies anymore. As I thought about this I did feel a sense of, "Good on ya", a sort of maturing had happened. It was very freeing in way to know that I was no longer bound to this. I was coming to understand what a master said in a book I read once. "Enlightenment is close when you sleep while you are sleeping." I am sure that is misquoted, but the idea of what was said comes through. When the master slept, he did not dream, nor did he travel, he slept. That for me is power.

I knew from this new awareness I was having that the next lessons I was to learn would be about self identity. I was looking forward to returning to my Toltec friends to hear their understanding of what self identity is. That evening I was invited back to discuss what I would come to understand as the illusion of self Identity.

I crossed the lawn, moving towards the giant stone table to find that comfortable spot where a small stream goes bubbling by. The water here was clear and fresh. It seems to be happy. The sounds it made as it travelled past you was like many small children laughing a giggling in a distance. A warm fun energy exuded beyond the liquid lusciousness. I sat in silence listening to the giggling water for some time before Teotihuan came to see what I was doing. He was very amused at my description of what the water felt like to me.

"So you have been wondering about self identity? Why is it that you are wondering? Do you feel you are in need of one?" He started giggling like the water as he asked me these questions.

"No, that is not it. I was talking with a friend the other day and he has some difficulties with his self identity. He is not sure that he knows exactly who he is. I remember very well feeling the exact same thing when I was younger. Now I have a much better idea of who I am, but I am not sure if that is really true or not. As I sit here and think about what my self identity is, I keep attaching who I am to what I do. So now I am not sure if that is really who I am or is it just what I do? So I was hoping we could talk about this?" I gave him the puppy dog eyes. Not that he ever fell for it but it made me feel like I had a little more say.

Teotihuan saw the puppy dog eyes, it made him laugh and shake his head, but he started to gather his thoughts as he readied himself to speak. "Really, puppy dog eyes, aren't we past that stage yet? At least you have a sense of humour. Self identity is a rather complex set of understandings in your reality. It is easily misunderstood as everyone has their own opinion of what it is or what it is supposed to be. In your reality you equate self identity with the ability to label who you are. That is both a good and bad thing in your mind. When you meet someone for the first time and they say, hi I am so in so, who are you? You usually respond with your name and often you throw in what you do for good measure, you know, so they won't think you are useless. What you are doing is tying your name to your work. You tend to develop a false sense of security by attaching yourself to those two things, your name and what you do. However for most people, the combination of these two things forms their self identity."

I was mulling this over in my mind as he spoke, remembering times I had introduced myself to strangers. He was right in how we introduce ourselves but I was not sure I agreed that this is how we identify ourselves. "I do not mean to interrupt, but speaking from my own experience here, many times when I have introduced myself I do exactly what you say, however I do that so I don't get into a conversation about who I really am. I use it as a convenience, not really as my personal identity."

He smiled and spoke,"Yes that is the flip side, you hide behind social conditioning. I do not mean that in a bad sense. However you are still identifying yourself but you are rebelling against common practices. The problem with self identity starts when you are not sure what part of yourself you are identifying with. Are you identifying with the physical you, or are you identifying with the soul? Some people identify with their mental selves, others with their emotional selves. This is how it gets very complicated, very quickly. There are no standards by which everyone is on an equal playing field to understand the rules of self identity. This is the chaos but it is also the answer. Are you keeping up?"

Well, I was never sure that I was keeping up even though I was hearing his words. I looked at him and nodded with a smile. He gave me that knowing look that said, "Non committal again, huh?"

"Ok so lets sort this out a bit, shall we? I want you to think on a personal level. What do you consider to be the self? Is it the image you project or is it who you are inside?" he spoke very softly, grabbing my attention.

Ok, I have never really been asked that before. "Well, if it is my self identity, I think it would have to be something more personal than what I project out there. Not that I lie in the way I project myself but I do not project all of myself all of the time, so what people see is like a hologram of the appropriate parts of me in the appropriate situation. So my self identity is attached to who I feel inside." I thought that was a marvellous answer.

"Very interesting, you actually said exactly what I was hoping you would say, that your self identity is ATTACHED to who you are inside. That is a very powerful point. So if this is true that your self identity is only attached to some part of you, then what is your self identity?" Teotihuan sat back on his hands, he was watching me as I searched my mind for an answer.

I really rather hated being put on the spot. I had come to understand that honesty was very forthcoming in the moment but it was not always well said or exactly what I meant. I knew I had to answer his question because he would not speak again till it did. He was stubborn as a goat even at 300 years old! So what is my self identity? I kept mulling it over and over in my mind and I honestly couldn't come up with a concrete answer. The only thing I came up with was that my self identity was the sometimes inflated ideas of who I believed myself to be all combined together. It is how I had to describe myself so that I did not get lost in the crowd. It is how I either wanted myself to be, or it is how I experience myself when I am looking at me through someone else's eyes. Yes that is it. Self Identity is how I feel about myself, but packaged in a description spoken as though I was looking through the eyes of an outsider.

"I think my self identity is always going to be false because it is not truly how I experience myself, it is what I believe myself to be as seen through the eyes of others. Is this true? I am just understanding right in this moment that the whole reason we feel the need for a self identity is to be able to define ourselves from others. The very fact that we are defining ourselves as apart from others, binds us to the definitions that others would put upon us. It is kind of hard to wrap my brain around this, but I think I actually understand. The only way to define yourself as separate is by first seeing yourself as the same.

So no matter what, you are never going to have an identity that actually defines just you. The best you can achieve is the illusion of a description based upon standards that are agreed upon by the consciousness of the time." I knew this was it. This was the illusion he was talking about. After all how can you describe the process of a soul inhabiting a body, words just don't cut it.

Teotihuan sat and smiled a knowing timeless smile. He did not nod or agree with me, he just smiled. "Your thoughts come from a deep place. Are you sure this is your answer?"

"Well it is the only one that makes sense to me at the moment. It may change down the road if you ask me again!" I was a little annoyed that he was questioning my thoughts, even though I recognized that his statement made me question my thoughts.

"It is a good answer. The fact that you need a self identity is proof of the Oneness. To have a self identity is very important in these realities. The Creator made all of us as an expression of itself so that we can experience ourselves in a unique way, and then the Creator has that experience within itself. Without self identity the Creator would experience the same thing through all individual expressions. In your reality the goal was to have a strong self identity so that you could stand out from others, be noticed and yet still be accepted. Without your individuality you would get lost in the sea of people. There are many reasons people get noticed and not all of those reasons are positive ones. Some people need to be individualized so badly that the means they use to get noticed, does not matter. They believe that they must leave a legacy to be of importance. So a strong self Identity is essential in your reality."

"In my reality self identity is important as well, but from a very different perspective. We, all of us here, understand that we are individuals and to be the best we can be is very important to us. However we are more aware that our greatness is important to the whole, to function as one. We have individuality but we see our individuality as a spoke in the wheel, not separate from the wheel. Here once we find our niche, we spend our lifetime developing it so that our greatness spills over onto all others to enhance their greatness. Our personal achievement is not personal. When we accomplish something our first thought is how we will all grow from it. We do not have the need to be great so that our identity will be seen. For us, our self identity is seen as inextricable from the whole. If we are great, then we are all great. The whole is a reflection of me, not the whole is better because of me. We are separate and the same all at once. This is most likely a difficult concept for you as of yet, but you are getting there. Some in your reality would try to call it a hive mind, but that is not an accurate description. We are not organized by one central mind, however we as individuals are very aware of our actions affecting all of what we are as a unit. Can you see the difference?" Again he sat back and waited for my response.

"Yes I really do see the difference and it makes complete sense to me. I can honestly say that I am not quite in the place to experience this in the way you describe it yet. I think the difference is, for you it all seems quite automatic. For me I would have to consciously start training myself to think in this way. In the 3rd dimension self identity is essential to the individual. In the 5th dimension self identity is essential to the whole. It sounds to me that the flow of energy changes. In the 3rd, what you put out comes back to you. In the 5th what you put out flows directly into the whole and you are affected by way of the whole more so, than by direct return action. Is this correct?" I sat staring at him, probably a little more intensely than I had intended because he started shifting in place.

"Exactly! Yes, the action is the same but the flow changes. In the 5th you are directly connected to everything around you, while in the 3rd there is a form of separation in how you affect what is around you. You still create your reality, but the flow is not so direct. Yes this is good that you have this concept solidly in your understanding. It is the one that most have a difficult time with when they first come here. They are expecting the delayed or separated reaction and it is not so pronounced here. It makes a lot of people feel they are out of control when in truth they have much more control over their reality. Initially it is a difficult time for most." I could tell he was thinking back to his arrival in this place and the chaos that ensued. I could feel the pain and distress emanating from him. The plant life around us seemed to wilt slightly as if they were crying with him. Even the colours seemed to dull slightly. Teotihuan was a powerful man, but now I could see with my eyes, just how powerful he was.

"Self Identity is the identity you believe yourself to be or the identity you desire yourself to be. It is not always the true energy of who you portray. This is one of the biggest reasons that the people in your world manifest what they think they do not want. It is difficult manifesting your dreams when you are working against your destiny. If you have a self identity that does not match your dreams or if your destiny is too far different from your dreams, it is very difficult to manifest. Someone who is not truly capable of seeing themselves as they are will have a hard time finding a dream to wrap around themselves. Any dream they come up with will always seem to elude them, and they will not know why. Material existence is highly valued in your reality. In and of itself there is nothing wrong with this, but if your true self identity is not focused on material possessions and you are working for nothing else, your work shall be in vain."

"You true identity can be found in who you are as a child. The more you can remember about yourself and who you remember yourself to be the closer you are to your true self identity. Now when most people remember their childhoods they focus on the events that happened both good and bad. Your reaction to the events that happened is not your true identity. Your true identity is the closest you can get to your soul while in physical form. It is the blueprint of who you had to be, to have the experiences you came here to have, so your soul could evolve. So finding your true identity may require that you peel off a few layers. Sometimes when people find their true self identity they are not happy with it because it doesn't fit the image they want for themselves. This can cause a tremendous amount of psychological and emotional separation to occur. Much of the mental illness in your world is based in this problem. So how do you find your true self identity? Yes I can feel that question forming in your mind. There are clues all over your reality if you choose to see them."

"Some find clues in the astrological charts, others pursue past lives, some look toward natural tendencies, there are many ways. However your self identity is divided into 8 pieces. A piece can be found in every one of your chakras. All you have to do is go into each chakra and make this statement. The statement is, My soul chose to learn about _____ through this pattern of belief. You can fill that blank with anything such as, relationships, money, love and even self empowerment. Now remember, your true self identity is the identity you were imprinted with to learn the lessons you came to learn. It will not match the identity you want your self to have. It is the key however to understanding the patterns in your life that shape your reality. You true destiny is to grow beyond the patterns, to shape them into the patterns you want them to be. True destiny is not about accumulation of anything it is about growing beyond the self you were born as. However the process of growing beyond the self often requires the pursuit of specific goals as a path of experience leading to understanding. So now you wish to have a process to discover what your identity is, so that you can go about shaping it?"

My brain was doing flip flops trying to make sense of all he had just said, even though it made perfect sense. It was as if the brain had gotten a bunch of words in the wrong order and it was trying to organize them. I just nodded at him deciding that was the safest way to respond in the moment.

Teotihuan could see my stress so he added, "This is a longer process than before so you may wish to record it on one of your devices. Take your time going through it. If you are not familiar with the chakra's you may want to do a little reading about them first. Do the process and then afterwards in a quiet moment take some time to assess which patterns are contributing to the challenges in your life. Create a plan to clearly change the pattern and then go back and do the process again. This time change the pattern that is creating a challenge, to how it would appear as an attribute in your life. Of course make sure you follow through with the plan in your daily life as well. You can choose to do all of the chakras at once or just one of them based on your current challenges. Always remember this visualization will show you the identity you came her with, not how you choose to perceive yourself. The identity you discover here, will allow you to make the changes you wish to create the life you want, and therefore create a self identity that is who you want to be. Now have fun with this and know that no matter what you discover, it is only there for you to decide if that is who you are or not. If you do not like what you see, then set about changing it. It is your life to do as you will."

Allow yourself now, to be in a place of rest, relaxation and safety. Let some music play gently in the background if you like. Sit or lay as you prefer. Close your eyes and relax. Breathe deeply and rhythmically. Breathe in and then release the breath slowly. Feel your body release all tensions. You are completely supported by the Universe. Continue to breathe deeply as your body drifts into a deeper state of relaxation. You mind is clearing and getting quiet now. You feel like you are floating on a cloud. You are warm and loved. As you drift into a deeper state of being, you allow yourself to become weightless, you are alert and the distractions of the outside world fade away into the distance as you experience your being in complete relaxation.

As you continue to drift along your awareness slowly, gently starts to focus on your root chakra. Feel the energy moving, spiralling in the colour of red. It is a vibrant strong energy that represents your material possessions, your physical body and your survival. Now focus on how you have manifested these things in your life and mentally make this statement, My soul chose to learn about survival and security through this pattern of belief. You may see images, hear words or have impressions. Allow all the information you need to understand your pattern around survival to come to you now. When you have what you need, release the pattern.

Return to that place of being aware in a relaxed state. Allow yourself now to focus on the second chakra, the sacral chakra. Feel the energy moving, spiralling in the colour of orange. It is a vibrant strong energy that represents your sexuality, your creativity and money. Now focus on how you have manifested these things your life and make this statement, My soul chose to learn about creativity through this pattern of belief. Allow all the information you need to understand your pattern around creativity to come to you now. When you have what you need, release the pattern

Return to that place of being aware in a relaxed state. Allow yourself now to focus on the third chakra, the solar plexus chakra. Feel the energy moving, spiralling in the colour of yellow. It is a vibrant strong energy that represents your personal power, your intellect and your understanding. Now focus on how you have manifested these things in your life and make this statement, My soul chose to learn about power through this pattern of belief. Allow all the information you need to understand your pattern around power to come to you now. When you have what you need, release the pattern.

Return to that place of being aware in a relaxed state. Allow yourself to focus now on the fourth chakra the heart chakra. Feel the energy moving, spiralling in the colour of pink or green. It is a vibrant strong energy that represents love of self and others and forgiveness. Focus on how you have manifested these things in your life and make this statement, My soul chose to learn about love through this pattern of belief. Allow all the information you need to understand your pattern around love to come to you now. When you have what you need, release the pattern.

Return to that place of being aware in a relaxed state. Allow your focus to move to the fifth chakra the throat chakra. Feel the energy moving, spiralling in the colour of sky blue. It is a vibrant strong energy that represents how we voice the truth of our thoughts and feelings and how aligned our head and heart are. Now focus on how you have manifested these things in your life and make this statement, My soul chose to learn about my truth through this pattern of belief. Allow all the information you need to understand your pattern around truth to come to you now. When you have what you need, release the pattern.

Return to that place of being aware in a relaxed state. Allow your focus to move to the sixth chakra the third eye chakra. Feel the energy moving, spiralling in the colour of indigo blue. It is a strong vibrant energy that represents how you see your reality and your intuition. Now focus on how you have manifested these things in your life and make this statement, My soul chose to learn about seeing reality through this pattern of belief. Allow all the information you need to understand your pattern around seeing reality to come to you now. When you have everything you need, release the pattern.

Return to that place of being aware in a relaxed state. Allow your focus to move to the seventh chakra the crown chakra. Feel the energy moving, spiralling in the colour of lavender. It is a strong vibrant energy that represents our connection with Creator. Focus on how you have manifested these things in your life and make this statement, My soul chose to learn about Creator through this pattern of belief. Allow all the information you need to understand your pattern around a Creator to come to you now. When you have all you need, release the pattern.

Return to that place of being aware in a relaxed state. Allow your focus to move to the eighth chakra above your head. Feel the energy moving, spiralling in the colour of white. It is a strong vibrant energy that represents how your physical reality aligns with your soul's purpose. Focus on how you have manifested this in your life and make this statement, My soul chose to learn about itself through this pattern of belief. Allow all the information you need to understand your pattern around your soul's purpose to come to you. When you have all you need, release the pattern.

Allow your understanding to come very clear now about the difference between your true self identity and the identity you wish to be. See how you can make simple changes in your patterns to succeed in doing this. Allow those changes to take place now in your awareness. Bring up two images in front of you, one is the image of your true identity and the other is the image of your desired identity. Look at them both and see how the true identity is starting to fade. It continues to fade until it has completely disappeared. You are now left with your desired identity. Your desired identity starts to move toward you, coming closer and closer. Stretch out your arms to this identity and embrace it. Allow yourself to absorb it completely into your body. Notice how it fits like a glove, you feel so comfortable in this identity. Allow yourself to settle into it as it settles into you. As this happens allow yourself this experience, I am grateful, I am healed, I am loved.

Now slowly start your ascent back to waking reality. Start to hear the sounds around you. Feel the air on your skin. Know that you are about to awaken to a new and wonderful life, and when you are ready open your eyes.

This session had exhausted me. I was ready to go home. My mind was still trying to absorb all of this and I thought it would be better absorbed if I was asleep. I often process better in dreams than I do with a waking mind. So I offered my thanks to Teotihuan and started back to my 3rd dimensional reality. I did not know what lay ahead, but the lessons seemed to be increasing in intensity. I was not sure I would make it through all this. For so long I held an image of the 5th dimension like it was a utopian society. It was not that. I could see how it was an idyllic place, but that idyllic place had to be created from the idyllic place in me and I was not sure I knew where that place was yet.

Chapter Seven

I could understand the necessity of these processes and starting the training procedures that would help the transition into the 5th, but I really just wanted to know more about who they were and what they did. I knew they were highly skilled masters at whatever they did, which from what I had seen included healing, the arts, inter species communication and much more. Every time I went there I ended up learning some new kind of intense process. I wanted to go there and have some fun. Maybe that was not possible but I knew these people loved to laugh, so I assumed they also liked to have a good time. I wanted to see what that looked like. So that was my next mission, to find out what their daily lives were like. If I was going to end up there, how would my life look? Was it even a life I wanted? I was hoping there was a way to find some of this out, before I signed a contract dooming myself to be disillusioned by a false imagining.

I returned to the Technicians and to my surprise it was dark. I had never been there at night before. I could see a large fire burning in the middle of the field. I followed the light and joined the group of faces that were lit by the fire. As my eyes adjusted to the contrast of dark and light, I looked around and was surprised to see all the homes were lit internally. I had just thought because they were such an ancient people that somehow technology hadn't found them yet. I was wrong. Some of the homes had light by their entrance doors as well. I was getting curious and knew I could not contain it much longer. I had just turned my body with the intent on going to check the light out and ran square into Teotihuan. He stood there giggling and shaking his head.

"Good thing I was not a jaguar. I have been standing there for some time waiting for you to finally give in to your curiosity." He could not contain his laughter. I wasn't sure why it was so funny that I ran into him but I welcomed the giggles coming from the old man.

"You have light!" I blurted out, followed by the embarrassment of realizing I blurted it out. I saw him furrow his brow and I wasn't sure if he could believe what he was hearing or that he couldn't believe I thought they were stone age people.

"Light? Yes we have light. Why would you think we would not have light? It is dark and we need to see." He was still sort of giggling under his breath.

"I don't know why I didn't think you would have electricity. I guess I just see you living such a simple and organized life. I never really thought about it, this is the first time I have been here at night. I had never noticed anything that would lead me to believe you had electricity. So I think I just assumed you didn't. Maybe I wanted to believe you didn't need it." I was realizing that I felt a little disappointed by how much they were like us at the moment.

"Electricity, no no. We do not have electricity. Our way of lighting the darkness is not what you know in your life. Come I will show you." We walked towards the home that had the light on outside of the door. As we approached I could see it was almost like a decorative statue. It looked to be made of natural elements and had been tiled in some kind of blue stone. It was quite skillfully done. Whoever had made it took great pride in their creation. It seemed to rise directly from the earth, like a tree root that decided it no longer wanted to be underground. Coming close to the top, at about eye level, there was a bowl shape. It was open on the top and had a ring around it that would slide to reveal different shapes that had been cut into the side of the bowl. Sitting at the side on a little shelf was a lid to cover the light. It had been so naturally built into the landscape, I just had not noticed it as something man made.

"Look inside the bowl and tell me what you see!" Teotihuan said to me.

I got on my tip toes and peered over the edge of the bowl. I did not know what I was looking at. I guess I had expected to see what was familiar to me, something like a bulb or a flame, but that is not what was there. In the middle of the bowl there was a hollowed out circular shaped clear crystal. It was hard to see past the brilliance of the light but in the hollow at the bottom of the crystal appeared to be a mix of powder. The light was streaming from the powder.

"Go on, pick it up" Teotihuan encouraged. I was nervous about that, thinking it would be hot. I very nimbly touched the edge of the crystal expecting to immediately retract my finger but it was cool to the touch. As I touch the surface of the crystal my finger tip appeared blue. I pulled my finger back and it was normal. I picked the whole light up and placed it gently in my hands. I was fascinated. Now the palms of my hands were turning blue. I balanced the crystal in one hand and the other palm returned to normal. I am sure my eyes were wide with wonder.

"Beautiful isn't it. Light is the natural by product of the combination of these three elements. Like sound is the by product of someone singing. When we first came here we were not sure, just like you, what we had gotten ourselves into. We actually thought this culture was more primitive than our own. When we were in your reality we relied on both fire and the gases that rise from the earth to supply our light. There were some that had learned how to work with crystals and produce minor amounts of light, but not like this. The powder you see is crushed stone from the caves. Blue and yellow stone, put them together and they do nothing, but put them in a crystal and gently tap the side long enough, and light is emitted. Of course it helps to ask for light and to be in the right state of mind, but this little amount of powder that you see there will burn for a year or longer. The lid is so we can contain the light and direct it through the cut outs on the side if we wish. There are times people do not want to be disturbed, so the slider acts as a message to anyone who comes to visit." Teotihuan stood there smiling, looking into the light. It seemed to take him to other places, memories were being unleashed.

"So what are the blue and yellow stones?" My enquiry jolted him from his moment of journey.

"All in good time. Learning is a process. If you learn something out of sequence it can cause you to stumble backwards. Much must come before, for you to understand why this works. At this point you may be able to understand it, but it would not truly make sense to you." He started back towards the fire, knowing if he stood there I would persist in my questions. He was wise.

"So you have come now to see what our lives are like? What do you think so far?" He sat with his back to the fire so he could see the truth in my face as it was lit by the flames

"Well, it is interesting. I am not sure I really have an opinion yet. I think many things that happen here are very magical. However I also wonder how you can do the same thing over and over again and not want to shoot yourself. I tend towards an endless curiosity and I am not sure that would stop. How do you do what you do and continue to love doing it?" I was very genuine in my question. My life had been such that I had never stayed in one spot for long, nor had I ever done the same job long term. Once I had done something enough, I got bored and wanted to go discover new worlds, and so I did. It always fascinated me, the people that lived in the same place for years or the people that retired from the job they had done for 40 years. I couldn't fathom it.

Teotihuan sat there laughing and trying to speak at the same time. So he gave into the laughing and waited for it to stop. Then after a couple of coughs as the result of laughing too much he began to speak.

"The life you describe sounds like a good life. You must have learned a great deal in your travels. You have experienced much that most would not get to experience. This is always a good thing. It prepares you for acceptance. So tell me now, what have you discovered in all of your curiosity driven expeditions?"

I sat down facing him and thought. "What have I learned?" After a few minutes of silence I could only thing of a couple of things. "I have learned that this planet is more than anyone can comprehend, and we will never know all the secrets. I have also learned that no matter how different people and culture's are, we are all the same." Yep that was it. That is all I had learned in 50 years of travel. That was pretty embarrassing to admit that in this moment.

Teotihuan once again sat there smiling that very knowing smile. "Now tell me, what you have learned about yourself.?"

I knew he was going to ask me that. Before the words fell past his lips I was already trying to think of the response. What had I learned about myself? I am not sure I had really thought about this before. I had always focused on what I had learned about where I went. Finally some realizations were coming to me.

"I have learned that the earth expresses her personality in different ways in different places and that I am very sensitive to those energies. I feel my way everywhere I go. I have learned that I can adapt very quickly to any situation, or I leave the situation. I have learned that loneliness is not real for me. I have learned that I really do have preferred places to live that are no where near where I was born. I have learned that ultimately people in general are a reflection of who I am, with the odd exclusion. I have also learned that I am getting tired of constantly moving, but I am terrified of being in one place. Oh and one more thing I have learned. I enjoy being in a place with a sense of history. A place where the land seems to want to share it memories with you. A place where she opens her hands to you and invites you in. The place also needs to be wild and natural. I need to be in the arms of the Great Mother to feel safe. Is that what you are looking for?"

"So you are telling me that you adapt quickly to a wild place that has loving energy and you don't normally get lonely?" He sat there with raised eyebrows waiting for my response.

"Yes that is a fair statement. But it doesn't feel like that is much to learn for the travelling I have done." It all felt a little empty when he put it that way.

"Let me help you. Your life has been divided into two parts. The life you have lived and the life you are about to live. You have spent the first half of your life looking for yourself through the reflection of other people and other places. Now as you go into the next part of your adventure you have realized that somewhere along the way you found you. Now you are preparing to be the mirror for everyone else. You are afraid that being still means that the excitement of discovery will no longer be part of your life. However doing life the way you do it is getting far too exhausting. You are really scared to leave behind the you that you have come to know, but you are feeling extreme pressure to embrace the you that you know you are becoming. You are praying that your sanity is intact because even though you are not travelling physically, you are travelling now in much more obtuse ways. You are afraid that you are going to become someone that even you don't recognize. Does that about cover it?"   He shrugged his shoulders and offered his hand in support.

"I think that pretty much covers it, yes. Maybe even add a little more in there around certain things, but yes that is the basics. Where did I find myself? I worked very hard at many things in my life that didn't go anywhere, and then all of a sudden I am back where I started and I know it is the right place to be and I cannot possibly be anything else. What happened with all that?" I stood there shaking my head, knowing he knew what I was talking about without needing to know the story.

"You are the personality type that has to investigate all possible scenarios before you can feel that you are making the right decision. You have always been that way. You are both the scientist and the experiment. It is only when you have exhausted all potentials in your mind that you will comfortably choose to reside where you thought you were not supposed to be. That is neither a good or a bad quality. It is simply you. I know you wonder why you have taken this path and others seem happy to never have left the safety of their home.

Well those people may truly be happy where they are or they may be too afraid to leave. They may also be afraid that they will find somewhere better and then be afraid to take the opportunity. In truth it does not matter because we are all on our own path. The important point to this is that you have aligned yourself with your destiny, that is why you are feeling the pull to settle into one spot now." Wisdom always seemed to exude from his words.

I have aligned with my destiny, what did that mean? I understood the words but I was unsure of what the ramifications were. I had spent many years looking for what I was supposed to do. I tried far too many jobs to remember. I moved to different places. I found many things I enjoyed but nothing that really stuck. Then I ended up emotionally back where I had started, in the realm of working with the unseen and unexplained. When I found myself there after many years of trying hard to not go there, I knew I had come home. I have not looked back since. I am comfortable in this world now, and happy to be here.

"Destiny is not something that you do, it is who you are. People in your reality are all looking for their destiny but they approach it like it is some kind of job. If you think your destiny is a job, it is unlikely you will discover it. Destiny is an alignment between your physical reality and your soul's purpose in your current incarnation. You can usually find clues to your destiny by recovering memories of the lives from which your current karma came. Your destiny and your karma are tied together. Albert Einstein said, You cannot solve a problem with the same understanding that created it. He is right and yes we are very familiar with Albert he is here in this place now. Destiny is the ability to solve an old problem in a new way. The old problem being your karma, and the new way being in your reality in your current time. So finding your destiny is a two part event. First you must discover the problems that have been plaguing you for lifetimes, and second you need to discover a new way to fix those problems. So destiny is not so much about what you do as it is who you are, and how you choose to express that in a way that often ends up being a form of occupation. Are you understanding this?" He was nodding his head as he spoke as if to encourage my acknowledgement of what I knew.

I was excited at this because I felt like I knew exactly what he was talking about. I had done some extensive past life work and saw the threads that ran through all lifetimes. My consistent problem was being comfortable with myself in positions of authority. I have very vivid lives of using and abusing power. In all of my lives that seemed to converge in my current life, I have always working in the unseen realms, sometimes using my talents for the people and sometimes using them against the people. But the running theme has been to be able to completely accept myself and trust my abilities in positions of authority. I knew Teotihuan knew that too.

"I do understand exactly what you are saying, and I would like to meet Albert Einstein as well." I said it matter of fact. I did not expect Teotihuan to start laughing again.

"Yes I am sure you would. However you do understand, until you move here permanently, your movements are restricted?" He laughed more and then continued. "So to discover your destiny you must do as you did and find the thread that runs through your life. Now if you have no idea of your past lives, you must look to the parts of your current life that consistently cause problems. Whether it be money or romance. Health or relationships. You will quite easily discover one or more areas that never seem to work for very long before they cause you stress. Once you discover those specifics then you must define your beliefs around those things. Do you believe that you are not worthy? Do you believe you are a better person if you are poor? Do you believe that life has abandoned you? Once you discover what you believe about your stressful ongoing situations, you can discover a direction for your destiny. You for example. You have spent most of your life dancing around your gifts and talents, never wanting to be responsible for what came out of your mouth, just in case you were wrong, until recently. Yes or no?"

"Yes for the most part. I was always shocked when I discovered I had been right about something, but inherently always knew it was the way it was supposed to be." I had to admit this to myself more times than I cared to remember.

"Right. Tell me know. When were you more likely to be wrong?" His eyes were piercing my soul now. I had better get this right I thought.

"I was most often to be wrong when a client had not liked what I said and had an emotional reaction. I would feel bad and try to shape what I saw in another way so they didn't keep hammering me. It was when I would go against my instincts or twist them in a way that they weren't pure somehow." I felt so ashamed when I said that. I hated it when people would ask for my help and then scream at me if I said something they did now want to hear, or cry and tell me they never should have called me. I felt so bad for them, I would hope that I was wrong and because of that my ability to see future events would get cloudy.

"Yes, it is hard dealing with people that don't want to know the truth. Many people get addicted to oracles because they are looking for the one that will tell them what they want to hear not what they need to hear. The job you do is a difficult one, no one contacts you because they are happily stoned on unicorns and rainbows." When he said that I got the distinct feeling it was personal for him. He said it with far too much empathy to not have experienced it.

"You have experienced the polarity of who you are. When you answer from your knowing, your are offering what people need. When you answer from emotion, you are offering what people want. So you can never make it personal, or it gets complicated. However to do what you do, it is all personal. I do understand the dilemma. However it also reveals your time line karma in your current reality. You have difficulty being and trusting when in a position of authority. However this has started to change for you. Tell me why it is changing?" His words were true, and I could see that he was allowing me to teach myself now.

" A few years ago I was at a place in my life where I knew I would die very quickly if I didn't change everything. It was hard but I changed everything and expected my problems to dissipate. I actually moved twice thinking I needed new starts, but the same old problems were there. It was then that I really understood that my external reality was not the whole problem. It did its part in contributing in a big way, but the root of the problem was with me. So I set about dealing with the problem. It was the onion process, you know, you peel a layer off at a time. Now I feel like I have whittled my problems away to where I am at the very root, the very core of each belief. I understand what my beliefs are and I understand what I have to do about it. That is part of my need to settle down as well. I can see how at the root it is all intertwined, and one belief cannot be fully resolved without resolving the others at the same time. At least in my case this is true. So yes, I am now about to launch myself into this." I knew when I said it, that not only did I understand it, but I actually meant that I was ready to deal with these core issues.

"So you are saying you are ready to step back into the eye of the people, as who you truly are, and trust that you will be safe in that situation?" I may have been wrong but I thought I felt a sense of pride coming from him.

"Yep, that is right. That is what I have spent the last couple of years preparing myself for. I know that is my Destiny. I now know as well, because of your gracious explanation, that doing this will clear my karma. It is scary because once the karma is cleared I no long have a point of relevance. I can see very clearly now how even though I hated having these issues in this life, they were also the anchor I used to base my self identity on. You just don't get one without the other, do you?"

I think I woke up at that moment. Something inside me clicked. I could see the interlinking between beliefs, destiny and karma and how it all had shaped my life. Letting go of it meant there were no more automatic moulds and I would have to do some conscious shaping if I was to re-anchor myself in a new life. That was both thrilling and terrifying. I could feel the weight of that responsibility.

" Now to answer the question we started this evening with, you wanted to know how we can do what we do over and over and not get bored? Here in this place we have released our karma, so we are no longer bound to solving old problems in new ways. Each one of us here has a talent that no one else can replicate, nor would we want to. In this reality we are completely aligned with our talents, it is like breathing for us. Since we are so aligned and we are not bound by a karmic structure, we have the continuous freedom to recreate how we do what we do. We work with our talent in one way till we are bored and then we shift reality in a way that it challenges us to use our talents in a different manner. I know it may be difficult for you to understand coming from a 3rd dimensional reality where the structure was put in place for you, but it is similar to shifting your perception to see something in a new light. What we do is shift reality so that our talents don't work well and we have to find a way to make them work. Kind of backwards but the same. This is what we have to learn to prepare us for 7th dimensional reality. Each dimension has it challenges. Think of it this way. You have travelled to many places to have the experience. What if you could stay still and shift realty so the place came to you. That is perhaps a better way of putting it. Will this suffice for you now?" Teotihuan was getting tired, it has been a long night and most had left the fire to return to their homes. I knew it was time for him to do the same.

"Yes thank you. I have learned a great deal here tonight. Will there be a process for this lesson?" I asked because that is the format I was getting used to.

"Yes in a way, but it will be different. Is that alright?" His voice was quiet now. It was time for me to go.

"Yes of course. Thank you so much. I hope you sleep well and have very pleasant dreams." I said my good byes and left the way I had come. I was getting a much better sense of the world he lived in. It seemed to me to be a world of extremes where the people were the bridge between the two. I went to bed that night wondering when I would get the process for discovering destiny. That morning when I woke, it was there.

Settle yourself into a quiet spot where you know you will not be disturbed. Have paper and pen handy as you may want to write things down. Allow yourself to relax and ask that your patterns clearly come into vision. You may remember some of your patterns from the last process. Keep them in mind, they may come in handy.

Do a quick scan of your life. Think back as far as you can, right into childhood if possible. Take note of the memories that pop loudly into focus. Make note of them. Now bring your focus back to your current moment. Over the last two years of your life, what has been a consistent problem for you. Money? Time? Relationships or lack of relationships? Try to be as specific as you can about the problem. Such as, if your problem is finding love, say something like this, "I have been on many dates but no one fits the bill. I am not sure I believe there are any good men left out there." Or "I work so hard but I am just making ends meet. I guess I am just not meant to have a good life."

Once you have written down all the statements you can think of, read through them. If you have several statements you will start to see categories emerge. You may have several statements about money but only a couple of statements about love. You may have mentioned health several times, while children are only mentioned once. It may help you to match the statements to the categories. The categories should be short, Money, Love, Family, Fear and so on. Now take a look at the statements you have written down. You are looking for similarities in your statements. Most of your statements may be fear based. Perhaps you are angry in most of your statements. Perhaps you find yourself playing the role of victim in your statements. Whatever similarity you find write it down on a separate piece of paper. This is the theme of your negative beliefs.

Now lets move on to something a little cheerier. I want you to look to what is right in your life, what you are happy with, or at least what is ok consistently over the last two years. It could be things as simple as I have great hair, or I finally found a job I like. It could be I just had a baby and I love being a mom. Perhaps something like this, I got dumped two years ago and I was devastated, however it turned out to be the best thing, cause I met someone new and now I am happier than ever.

Follow the same process for these statements, look them over if there are several and see if you can divide them into categories. Place each in its category and then look for similarities in the statements. Find what is similar and when you do turn it into a statement and write it on the same paper you wrote your negative belief theme on.

Now lets look at the stuff in your life that you may do as a hobby or just because you love doing it. Some may be passionate about certain things, others may just have a healthy curiosity. Take a look at your life and ask yourself is there anything you do for pleasure or enjoyment that you have had an ongoing love affair with all your life? Maybe yes or maybe no. If not then ask yourself this question, what would I continue to do in my life even if I was not being paid to do it? Still nothing? Ok well here is my last suggestion. When you allow yourself to daydream about your ideal occupation in life, what are you doing? Describe these things in as much detail as possible. Something like this. When I daydream I see myself on a yacht sailing the ocean. The seas are calm and the food is good. I have a couple of companions with me and I feel safe and happy. We go into every port of call and shop in all the small boutiques by the wharf. We buy all the supplies we need for the next leg of our journey and have a decadent meal before we leave. I never tire of the sunsets, no two are alike. The sound of water moving against the boat lulls me into a beautiful dreamless sleep.

Describe what you see in your imagination with as much emotional and physical detail as possible. Now look through the statements you made about what is right in your life. Again look for any similarities you can find. You may find this in the emotional description or in similarities of what you are doing in your dream and what you are doing that is right in your life. All of these things are clues for you. Write down any similarities you may find and any understandings you may be having about your patterns in this moment. Write it all down because some ideas can be very fleeting.

Now with fresh eyes go back and look at what is wrong in your life. Look at the patterns and beliefs you have discovered that do not make you happy. How different is your dream, from what is wrong in your life? How far apart are your dreams and the things that are wrong in your life? Write down any or all insights you have about your dreams versus your negative patterns.

You should now have a tally of what is not working in your life, what is working in your life and what your dreams are. This is all you need to determine your destiny. Now we are going to ask one last question before we figure out our destiny. Looking at the things that are wrong in your life and the things that are right in your life ask yourself this question. How does it serve my purpose that I have created this polarity in my life?

Here is what I mean. Two ongoing problems I have had in my life are my weight and my finances. Being overweight started in childhood as a way to feel safe in my environment. It was my armour. However as an adult the threats are gone but the weight stayed. Yes it had become a habit, but it had become way more than that. It had become my excuse not to participate in life. It was a great reason to not put myself in situations where I might feel vulnerable or make mistakes. No I did not say I could not do this or that because of my weight, but it was what I was thinking when I turned down many invitations.

Finances were always an issue growing up. There just wasn't any money. When I got old enough to make my own money I found myself to be very driven and I would give it everything I had to make money in minimum wage jobs. I was great at saving and being fugal. But I never had a lot of money. As I got older my finances started to fluctuate even more, having a nice chunk in the bank to being to broke for long periods of time. When I finally had the courage to ask myself what purpose this is serving for me, I realized that I associated money with stress, pressure and the expectation of others. As I got older I was capable of making much more money because I had invested in my talents and had become a very capable person.

For me it was a double edged sword. Putting myself out there would mean the money would come, but it would also mean that I would be subject to greater pressure and expectation. Being poor in my eyes, protected me from being vulnerable to the opinions of others. It was also a great reason to not participate in life.

That is when I saw it. I saw the pattern. The things that didn't work in my life didn't work because I as a way to protect myself from vulnerable situations. If you are new to this kind of thinking, this may all sound pretty crazy to you. So I encourage you to ask that question of yourself, :"How does it serve my purpose that I have created this pattern in my life?" Be as honest as you possibly can, no one has to see your answers, only you know the truth. Once again make a list of how these patterns serve you emotionally and look for the common emotion that will emerge from them. This emotion is your hot button. My hot button was vulnerability. Whatever your hot button is, it will play a huge role in your destiny. At this point you may be flooded with memories of this emotion pattern in your life. You may have lots of sudden understandings all at once. This is just confirmation that you hit on the right emotional pattern.

Once you have done this it is time to put it all together. Remember that for this process the definition of destiny is to be able to solve an old ongoing problem in a new way. Once this problem is solved the barriers between what you fear and what you desire can be removed.

So what pattern do you see emerging from the pages you have written on? How does this pattern prevent/protect you from something? Are you ready to release the pattern for good? Are you willing to take the needed steps to release the pattern? Do you feel it is safe for you to release the pattern? Once you have answered all these questions it is time to let go of what no longer serves you.

In the past I have thought that releasing a pattern was as simple as changing my mind about it, seeing it from a different perspective. Sometimes that is very true. I can work for patterns that are not deeply ingrained. For patterns that have been continuously reinforced in your life over decades the process can be a little more involved. For instance, when I was going through the process of discovering my own patterns I started to realize I was walking on my heels. This surprised me because I had always been someone that walked on the ball of my foot. I tried to follow the time line backwards to when it started and I discovered it was initiated during a three year court battle with my ex. It didn't take much to figure out the symbolism. I walked on my heels because I was backing away from life, trying to keep myself safe. I no longer wanted to do that so I consciously started walking on the balls of my feet again. Yes there were a few days of sore muscles just from the adjustment in balance, however I also noticed that I seemed to suddenly become willing to meet things in more of a head on fashion. Walking on the balls of my feet was symbolic for leaning into life, not away from it. That very simple act helped me shift my entire life.

When you are trying to release a pattern it is essential to pay close attention to the details. Little things like how you walk can make a big difference in how successful you will be in achieving your goal. So now you have decided what your pattern is and you are ready to release it, now what do you do? First and most importantly have compassion for yourself. Understand this release may take some time to accomplish and love yourself through it all.

Your emotional hot button is the key to releasing your pattern. Go through your pages till you find your one word emotional hot button. Mine was vulnerability, so we will use it as an example. Once I discovered this was my hot button I started a practice of consistently checking in with myself throughout the day to discover how vulnerable I felt at any given time. On a scale of 1-10 I would rate everything I did throughout the day. I discovered that most things I did that involved other people, made me feel a certain level of vulnerability. If I was in the middle of the bush, I felt safe. With this understanding I was able to define my vulnerabilities even more.

My daily practice was based on two questions, "How vulnerable do I feel in this moment?" And the other question was. How can I make myself feel powerful? Some of the responses I received about how to make myself feel powerful did not always make sense. However I trusted my instincts and followed through. Sometimes they worked and sometimes they didn't. However I did learn how to grow beyond my vulnerabilities. Simply by acknowledging what I felt in the moment I allowed myself to be present enough say, "I was OK." Sometimes that was all it took. As long as there was no threat to life and limb, I was able to tell myself "I am OK, everything is fine."

If you can make a practice of working with yourself in this manner you will teach yourself to see things as they are and not as you are anticipating them to be.

We are all human and all addicted to our habits. If we rush into anything to fast we will just end up replacing one habit for another, or one hot button for another. The most powerful part of this journey is the compassion you must show for yourself. Remember you have been conditioned in this way for years, maybe even decades. It will take a little time and persistence to wean yourself from the pattern, but you can do it, all you have to do, is love yourself through it.

Chapter Eight

Letting go was often a theme in my life. However letting go was not something that was favourably taught in this society. No, this society was more inclined to teach you to grab on to something and no matter what, never let go, never give up, never say die. Unfortunately for us, we somehow transferred our deliberate persistence in pursuing goals into the inability to let go of anything at all. Yes, I know those people too, the ones that are constantly cleaning their closets and giving away everything they had to charity, but were they letting go of the clutter that was inside of them? Were they acting on the outside what they should have been doing on the inside? There is no way of ever really knowing what is going on with people. Our society was not a society that was fond of people freeing themselves from their situations, physical or emotional, to replace pain and suffering with joyous experience.

The focus was always on what you should have, or what you should be. We are preached at constantly how things are always in a slump but if you tried to better yourself, the truth is you could actually make it worse. Media taught us we were no one if we weren't rich, pretty and powerful. However the media never explained why so many of those rich, pretty, powerful people did not seem to be very happy. Buying into the elitist attitude that the media preached led to destruction for many that tried to grab the brass ring. It made me wonder why? If that lifestyle is so magnificent why are so many of them badly addicted, depressed, stressed and not happy? However when you look at some of the poorest people in the world, they have no real material possession but they are very happy as a society as long as their basic needs are taken care of. What was going on?

My answer was not long in coming. I had taken a few days off from the Technicians and the teachings they were offering me. When they knew I was getting too tired or to much was getting neglected in my life, they would ban me from coming to see them. No matter how hard I tried to gain access, the door would not open. That is what had happened in the last few days. Then I heard Teotihuan's familiar voice in my head and I knew it was time to return. That evening I lay down and allowed myself to drift between the world's, landing in the familiar court yard near the massive stone table. I was back, part of me always wanted to say, "I was home".

"Welcome back. Were you able to get things done in your life?" Teotihuan's unusually warm greeting caught me a little off guard.

"Ya, I guess so. I am not sure that I was able to do everything I was supposed to do because sometimes I am not sure what I am supposed to do." I started to laugh. I know my statement sounded a little crazy but it was true. There were times I felt like I should be doing something but I had no idea what.

Teotihuan's furrowed brow told me I was in for a lesson. I wasn't sure if he didn't understand what I had said or he disapproved of what I said, either way I was now regretting saying it.

"What do you mean you do not know what you are supposed to be doing? I am not sure I understand the meaning of this?" Yep there it was, the question that I would now attempt to answer only to find out that I knew what I thought I didn't know all along.

"Well I know all the physical stuff I am supposed to do. You know, eating, sleeping, cleaning up after myself. But there is always more than that. There is always that nagging feeling that I should know more, or being doing something else to get where I want to go. In truth it is exhausting. There is never quiet in my life. Something always feels like it needs attention. That is why I like coming here. When I am here I know my phone won't ring and there won't be any messages coming in. Even though we talk, it is very quiet here. Don't misunderstand me. I love the constant interaction with everyone but when it stops for a short period of time, I feel like something is wrong. Even when I have down time I spend it obsessing about how not to have too much down time." I started laughing again. Hearing myself say it in that way, it sounded so ridiculous.

"So you are not in your life, you are like the energy in your life. You keep directing it to go here and there but you can get nothing done because no one is really present to do it. Your life is an illusion if you are not present in it. You constantly think about your life, you do not really experience your life. There is a gap between where you are and where you want to be? You fill that gap with thoughts of how to get there but they all disappear like a mist. Thought without action is unfulfilled. Action without thought is reckless. Action and thought must come together for creation to happen. You are not in your own life, we have a name for this, we call it being a Ghost. Ghost's are stuck between two realities, not in one world or the other. They think they belong in one spot when really they belong in another. Is this the problem, are you a Ghost?" He sat a smiled at me. Knowing that I would react, he was always a few steps ahead of me in the conversation. I had often wondered if he could hear every word I thought, but I had no proof this was true. I expect it was just wisdom from his many years of teaching.

"I am not sure I would think of myself as a Ghost, but I do understand your meaning. I have had amazing moments in my life of being totally present in what I was doing, but they never last very long. However I can see how you would compare my life to that." I responded instead of reacting and I could tell that pleased him.

"I am not talking about you just being present in your life. I am talking about you actually participating in your own life so that you are not using your body as a robot to accomplish things on a daily basis. The first time you came here how did you feel?" He stopped, cocked his head to the side and waited.

"Oh well after I got over the initial confusion, I would say I felt like I was in a piece of heaven. Everything was so alive and vivid. The sounds and the smells were almost overwhelming. I loved every second of it." I hadn't thought about that first visit in awhile, it made me feel warm all over.

"Right and now you do not see any of the things you saw the first time you were here. Do you know why this is?"

"I guess it is familiar now. I am comfortable here. Maybe not so comfortable in this moment but normally." I laughed trying to let him know that I learn better in a little levity.

Teotihuan laughed in return. He received my message and I could see him physically relax. There were times when he could forget himself a little too. Now he was in a better place to teach.

"Yes familiarity. I too have gotten familiar with you and as you just saw, perhaps I have come to place some expectations on you. I do apologize. But tell me now. What is familiarity? What is it to you?" This time he sat back relaxed, intending on a conversation, not a lecture.

"Familiarity? I don't think I have ever really thought about what it means to me, I have always just used it as a word. I guess it is a word I use almost as an excuse to not pay attention. Or sometimes I use it as a word to not have to get into a long conversation about something. But mostly I guess I use it as a short cut, like, I am familiar with this or I am familiar with that, so people don't have to describe something I think I already know. It is a word that creates a faster way to get where I am going in a conversation." I was happy with that description.

"That is very insightful. I think it is true of most people. Being familiar with something means they can basically dismiss that thing in their pursuit of something else. However very often something that people think they are familiar with turns out to be not so familiar. Can you think of any occurrence's of this in your life?" I knew he was leading me to something, I just wasn't sure what.

"Oh ya for sure. It happens a lot. Especially if someone is giving me directions to a place I haven't been in a long time. I will say something like, I am familiar with the area. Then when I get there it has changed so much I have no idea where I am. When I am having a conversation with someone and I tell them I am familiar with a concept, then later I find out they had a very different idea than me about the same thing. So in the end I was not familiar with their interpretation. That can be really embarrassing." I was regurgitating memories now of moments of embarrassment, when I heard Teotihuan clear his throat to get my attention.

"Ahem, I guess I am familiar now too?" He was laughing out loud now. He just loved the feeling of making his point without speaking. "Sometimes being familiar is convenient and sometimes it can be a bit of a disaster. What happens when you become too familiar with your own life? Based on your description you basically bypass it to get somewhere else. Is this true? And where is it you are trying to get to?" Again he waited for me to speak

"I guess you are right, I have just never thought of it like that before. Where am I trying to get to? Well sometimes it would be whatever goal I had laid our for myself, other times I probably don't know. I just know I am not supposed to be where I am. Even though I may not be sure of where I am going. I know that sounds crazy but it is that way where I am from. So many of us are rushing to get away from where we are, to get to a place we have been told that we should want to be." Again I was having problems hearing what I was saying. I must have sounded like a complete nut. I wasn't sure if he could even understand any of this. The world he lived in was so different. From what I knew there was no where to go and why would they want to.

"Yes that is exactly how my reality was too, just before we ascended. It was a painful way to be in our lives. We were not living we were going from excuse to excuse hoping it would take us too where we though we should be. Most times follow the same pattern though they do it in different ways. Your world is so consumed by everything outside of themselves that they vacate their own lives. That or they become so consumed with everything outside of themselves that they hide in their own bodies, never actually participating in their lives. Either way it ends up being the same. A life lived outside of the self, is a life you pass through without making any stops. In the end you never know how you got to where you are, cause it is all a blur. The question you have to ask yourself is, why are you trying so hard to get somewhere else?" I could see the pain in his eyes and hear it in his voice as his own memories took him back to his life in a 3rd dimensional world. I sometimes forgot that he was once where I am. I made a promise to myself not to forget this again.

"How many times have you rushed to get somewhere else and discovered that it was not where you wanted to be either. I do know the answer to that so you don't have to tell me. All that time you spend out of your body, it is as though you believe you can create your future with only a thought. You take your awareness and retreat to your mind not allowing yourself to fully experience the senses of the body. After so many years of doing this you wonder why you can't feel anything or when you do move into your body you are overwhelmed by all the intensity. That leads you to seek something to either make you feel or to make you stop feeling. This is how so much substance abuse begins. Do you realize emotion can only be felt in your body? You cannot feel it in your mind. The people in your reality are not encouraged to be in their bodies, to love their bodies. They are not taught that their bodies are an amazing well spring of information that is designed to extract everything from your surroundings and filter it so the brain can make sense of it. The body also receives and sends information to whatever is in our surroundings. Without being present in your body, you will not receive 90 percent of the information that is there for you. Even if you are an expert telepathic, you still need to use your body as a broadcaster for the energetic waves you are sending. The media in your dimension drives people farther and farther from their bodies, because of the obsession with perfection. Those that do not think they are perfect want to abandon their bodies, and often they set about trying. You cannot be in your life without your body. The more issues you have with your body, the less you are in your life, period." Teotihuan made a strong hand gesture at the end of that sentence. This was something he was passionate about. I hadn't seen him like this before. Normally he was so balanced and controlled when it came to his emotions. I wondered what was behind it.

"You body is a very magical thing. It is the only place you can feel who you are. Thought is the blueprint. The house that you actually live in, is your emotions. Emotions are incredibly powerful and it is wise to have control over them, but do not try to erase them. The movie the Matrix that you liked so much, if you remember all the people in the pods that were producing body heat to make power for the machines. Well if that were a true scenario the machines would have developed a way to evoke emotion and capture that for power, it would make much more sense. Emotion is the creative energy. When you abandon your emotions you abandon yourself. When you abandon yourself you are not in your life. In the same, when you are not in your life, you abandon yourself. One is inextricably linked to the other. Many people that are overweight, are that way because they are not involved with their body. If they start practising being in their bodies they then discover their emotions and what they have separated themselves from. Tell me something. Why do you not feel safe in your body?" He was calming down again. The emotional burst was over and he moved through it in a seamless way.

"Why do I not feel safe in my body? Well, I think it is because I am not sure that I can trust my body to be there for me when I need it." That was as honest as I knew how to be.

"This is a pattern in your life isn't it. You wonder if you can trust your car. You wonder if you can trust your relationships. You wonder if you can trust that money will be there for you. However all of these things are not so much about trust as they are about maintenance. Your car is more reliable if maintained properly. Your relationships are better with maintenance. Money needs maintenance as well. So do your emotions and your body. You are in control of your life and you are responsible for the maintenance. However if you are not in your life, there is no one there to do the maintenance. Are you starting to see the vicious cycle that comes from not participating in your own life." A big sigh exploded from him. For some reason that conversation had taken a lot out of him.

As for me. I can honestly say I had a few light bulbs go on in my brain. Anytime you try to escape something in your life, you also abandon part of your body. The less aware you are of your body, the less you can feel your life. The less you feel your life, the less control you have over it. You have to be in your life to shape it the way you want it to be. Not participating in your life is self abandonment, cause in the end we only live in our bodies, and we can only experience our life though our body. So, note to self, find ways to be in my body as often as possible. One more note to self, do not use substances to force myself into my body.

A great way to experience being in your body is by spending time outside with your shoes off. Take the time to ask questions of your body. Ask your feet what they feel when the grass touches them. Ask your skin what it feels when the breeze caresses it. Ask your hair what is feels from the sun. Ask these questions of all parts of your body. You may get some interesting answers, do not dismiss them. Different parts of your body experience reality in different ways. You can also go through the different parts of your body and ask, what emotion lives here. You may find that your nose holds curiosity, while your knees hold intention. Again expect some interesting answers. Take your time to get to know your body. Start treating it as though your life depends on the partnership you create with it, because you know what, it does. But most of all, be kind, be compassionate and be accepting. You are the only you that has ever been on this planet. Never before and never again will there be another you, and I believe that is pretty special and pretty powerful. Treat yourself like you believe it too.

Make sure you are participating in your life. Life can get crazy and it is easy to lose focus. Every now and then try to take a minute and think about the last week of your life. How much of it did you do for you? Did you spend all your time taking care of other people's needs? Did you do nothing but work? Don't try to justify it to yourself that work is not about someone else. Come on, really? If it really was for you and you loved it so much you wouldn't classify it as work would you? Just try to make sure every week you take some time and put you in your life. While you are doing that, you may as well be fully in your body experiencing reality and that way you can kill two birds with one stone. If you need to be addicted to something, then being aware of your body would be a good thing to develop into a habit. Just think of what you could accomplish if you were aware of what you were doing all the time. Life is meant to be enjoyed for the most part. If you are not participating in your life, then you are not enjoying the life you are in. Give yourself permission to tweek your life just a little. Tweek it enough to put a smile on your face everyday, that is all it will take.

Chapter Nine

"Where do you live?" The question was sudden and caught me off guard. I really believe Teotihuan enjoyed this. He believed he got the most truthful answers along with their Freudian slips when he caught me focused in another direction.

"What do you mean, where do I live? You don't mean where as in the house or the location do you?" I already knew he didn't I was just buying a little time to formulate an answer.

"Quit buying time and answer the question." He looked at me and laughed. I guess I was just to obvious

"Well I am still not really sure what you mean. Do you mean what is my stance on this or that? Do you mean where is my heart? That is such a vague question, it could mean anything." I was protesting because I really wasn't sure what he was specifying. He thought he was being specific but I just couldn't hear it.

"You are familiar with the concept that you live on a planet, live in a house and live in your body. Yes? Well I am asking you where you live in that body? In your body there are eight rooms. Which one do you live in? Or do you live in all of them equally?" His eyes were bright and inquisitive. He was on the edge of his seat waiting for me to answer. I guess someone had eaten his Wheaties today.

"Ok see, now you just lost me. Eight rooms in my body. I don't even know what that is. How is it you are always expecting me to answer questions that I have no reference for?" I was a little annoyed but more than that, I took great delight in yanking his chain too.

"Ok, truce. I just wanted to see if you would know what I was talking about or not. Just seeing how far along you actually are on this journey. Don't get defensive."

"Well it would make more sense if you had said 7 rooms. I would be familiar with that. Seven Chakra's, spinning wheels of light. You work with them all the time." I had an idea where he was going with this but decided to play dumb a little longer.

"Eight!" He said this very firmly.

"Eight, what?" I questioned.

"Eight Chakra's. You have eight chakra's." Now he seemed to be getting a little annoyed. Yes, I was feeling like I might just have the upper hand. Then the next thought I had was, no, every time I think I have the upper hand, it gets slapped. Back to playing dumb.

"What do you mean I have eight chakra's? All the literature talks about seven. There are lots of little ones too but they don't talk to much about them. I have always wondered about that. Maybe size really does matter." I started to laugh, but I don't think he got the joke cause he looked at me with a bit of a scowl. So I stopped laughing. Then he broke out into a big belly laugh, looked directly at me and said, "Who has the upper hand now?" I just shook my head. There was the slap.

"Yes traditionally you are right. You have had seven acknowledged chakra's. However as you evolve you evolve into opening the eighth chakra and expressing it through you body. I call the eight chakras the eight rooms of your life. You will also be opening up some new small chakra's as well. Some chakra's will be merging, some will be expanding, some will be collapsing. This is why it is important to know where you live, because it will affect the balance of the chakra's and how they operate in your body. Do you understand now that I have explained it fully?" He was still chuckling under his breath.

"Yes thank you for explaining it." I said that in my most dignified voice. Then I bowed and placed my hands together in front of my heart as though he was my guru. He kind of huffed and swished his hand at me, he knew I was making fun.

"Your body is an incredibly powerful tool. Not only does it give you a place to live for your lifetime, it also does battle on your behalf on a daily basis. You probably know more about the security on you computer than you do the security in your body. Your brain records all information that you do not have time to pay attention to. It is stored in what you would think of as files attached to events. The files are categorized based on the information gathered. Things like emotional, verbal and visual. That is why sometimes when you recall a memory you do not get the whole sensual experience you had in the moment you had it. You did not recall all the files at the same time."

"Your body is also a sensory receptor. I receives all energetic information around you as well. Most people only acknowledge this when they feel something they cannot explain. Everyone has had that experience and few ever discover the proof of what they feel. So if there is no proof, they dismiss their feelings as imagination or reaction to something else. As you will come to understand, paying attention to what you feel can be the difference between life and death. Your body is something you have come to take for granted and most abuse it daily over long periods of time and wonder why it is breaking down. Sometimes they wonder why they can't feel the same way they used to, or they just don't remember things like they once did? Your body, like your planet will only take so much before it rebels. If it is still functional enough and wishes to stay alive, it will send you messages in the form of some kind of discomfort, pain or disease depending on how easy it is to get your attention. The disease is not the problem, that last many years of your life is. So we are going to spend a lot of time talking about the body and the transition it will go through from its perspective. Are you OK with this?" Teotihuan sat looking at me directly. I could feel him sending something to me, but I was not sure what it was. There was a definite feeling, like a gentle pulsing hitting my torso in a wave like fashion. I looked down at the front of my body and then I looked at him. He was smiling, he knew when I did that, I was feeling what he was doing even though I had no idea what it was.

"I am not sure what all that was about, but yes. I would love to talk about the body and how it is going to be affected through all of this." The front of my body now had tingles all up and down it, and I felt nothing in my back. I could see this would probably be a very interactive module in my learning and I wasn't sure if I liked that or hated it.

"I am going to start here because it is always a good idea to have a strong foundation to build on. Now listen very carefully, what I am going to tell you will change your life if you don't filter it. Ready? Your body does not lie! Your body is not designed to lie. It has no filters for lying. For you to receive a message through your body that you think is a lie, you have filtered it through your ego. Let me say that again. Your body does not, has not, and never ever will lie to you!" He was so emphatic about this. He was sort of rocking back and forth as he banged his fists into the soft ground beneath him. Obviously another touchy nerve point for him.

"Ok, I got it. My body does not lie. I know that means a lot more than I am giving it credit for now, but I look forward to you explaining it to me." I knew I had to say something. He needed to know I heard him but he also needed to know, that I really did not fully understand what the heck he was talking about.

"No, you don't really got it." He started to laugh. "You want to got it but you don't really got it, at least not yet. Your body is really what you would think of as an organic computer. The hard drive is your DNA. Your software is your belief systems, This is how you create a life for yourself, with these three things. All you ever have known or need to know is in your DNA. Your beliefs are the filters you use to colour the world the way you need it to see it, to learn the lessons you came here to learn. Your body is the tool you use as a balance between the two extremes. Your body and the information it is designed to give you is where you need to learn to place your trust. I remember how it was for us before we ascended, everyone was looking outside themselves for the answers. Now this is not always a bad thing, you can gain valuable insight and direction by looking outside yourself, however you can only gain truth by looking into yourself. Always remember your dimension is designed to be very flexible with the thing you call reality. In your dimension there is no one reality, there are only overlapping agreements that allow everyone's to experience their own version of reality. It is only in this way that you can come to experience what reality is. You must learn to stop looking through the filters of everyone else's reality and experience yours, through your body. Now do you understand?"

His voice was soft and quiet. Sometimes as he spoke, images seemed to paint themselves in my mind, so my understanding was complete. This was one such moment. I felt calm and relaxed, almost lulled into a space of floating, detached from my own understanding, and instead floating through the meaning that flowed on Teotihuan's breath.

"Ok are you back now? We need to move on with this. Time is shifting and this needs to be done before it shifts too far. So your body is the intermediary between the higher realms and the realm of illusion you choose to create. Without your body none of this would be possible. Remember from our earlier lessons that the DNA is both a receiver and a sender of information, however it works through the energy systems of the body to do this. So if for any reason you think you live somewhere other than your body, you might want to change that perspective. I have never been able to truly understand how so many people can navigate their lives and not be consciously aware of their bodies. I think this is why your society is so entranced with Zombies. I laugh because when people are not aware in their bodies that is exactly how they experience their reality. They are in it, but they are not in any way connected to it. Fascinates me. In other times, if you were not connected to your body, you would get eaten by something bigger and hungrier than you. Oh that's right it still happens to you in your society, except the thing that eats you is not covered in fur with big teeth, it is called your life. Yes, that is right, if you are not consciously connected to yourself, you will be consumed by your own life, out of control, with no idea how you got there. This disease is called denial. And that is not where you want to be." Teotihuan was very animated right now. I was enjoying this rather unusual display of emotion from him. I could tell that this subject was very important to him, and I could see why.

In our society we are so disconnected from our bodies. So disconnected in fact that we have no idea who we are. We see our bodies in the mirror and hate them. We want them to be something different than they are. We have taken this problem to the extreme and it has filtered down into our beliefs in such a way that we have no sense of self now. We have looked in the mirror for so long and not connected to our body that we can not see ourselves. We do not identify with our body and therefore can not find our soul. We judge our bodies, and because we do not truly connect to them we badly abuse them with all varieties of substances and emotion. We hide in the very bodies we do not want to see, and complain when someone else can't see us. Because of what Teotihuan was drilling into my head, I was starting to understand how being disconnected from our bodies had left us a spiritually deficient society. How can we believe we are infinite souls if we can't connect to the body we live in now? You have to go through the body, to find the soul. Becoming conscious of your body was the first step in self acceptance, but it was the step that would ultimately take you anywhere you wanted to go.

"The time is coming very quickly where your body will be the tool you use to navigate your life. You will use it as you use your car. You may be very attached to your car, you may love your car and take very good care of it, however you understand you are not your car, so you choose to consciously direct your car where you want it to go. You car does not have an autopilot button with the option to go wherever it chooses to go. However that is how most people live in their bodies right now. Their bodies are on autopilot and they do not consciously participate in most decisions that are being made. If you are going to succeed at using your body as a highly developed organic computer that you are dependent on for all your input and output, then you need to start feeling your body. In the times to come your body will be something you can use as a creator or as a weapon. It is the tool you will use to change the reality that is around you, to be what you desire it to be. Right now the reality that is around you, is controlled by the agreement that you made with Mother Earth as a mass consciousness. Yes there are interruptions being created in the agreement but that is something that you agreed to as well. In the 5th dimensional reality, your agreement is direct, the Earth is not the middle man. So if you are not working in unity with your body, you will not be able to consciously direct the energy you project to shape your reality. Understand?" I could tell he was wanting a break. The intensity that was coming from him was enormous. Quite frankly, I was getting tired too.

"Yes I understand what you are saying, even though I am not yet aware of how this will happen, it makes complete sense to me." That was the honest truth. I could feel what he was saying was true, but at this moment in time I had no idea how to operate my body at the level he was talking about.

"You are entering a period of accelerated consciousness on your planet now. We are going to talk more about this. There are symptoms and they should be mentioned. Learning to connect to your body, and from that point of connection, to manage your energy is essential not only in your growth but for your survival. Right now you count 7 continents, one for every chakra. You are moving to an 8 chakra reality, that means you are one short. This is something you may want to think about. Where is the other continent going to come from? This is what so many of you feel rising in you. The Earth has always maintained land masses based on chakras. Although these are not meant to be confused with the Earth's actual chakra points. Give this much thought, I know you find it intriguing. Now I am old and I am tired. Go home and let me get some sleep!" He kind of wobbled as he raised himself from the ground. He was laughing so hard he could barely walk. I had thought many times of what an enigmatic speaker he would have been in my reality.

I wasn't really sure how to file that last statement of his. He was implying that something would rise, another land mass. Earth changes in full force. As I thought more about this, I really started to wonder about how much our body was mirroring what was going on with Earth's body. We were after all, made of her flesh and tuned to her frequency. Over the last 20 years I have had many visions about what was to come. Some visions stay the same and some change. It only makes sense to me that something has to happen and our level of consciousness will determine the level of distress we go through. What he said did frighten me on some level. It only frightened me because I have been given many of my own signs of late about the next step in my life. I have an obsession with being up high. Living in a high spot with solid rock beneath me. At this moment I live a coastal existence and it is time to move. I also want to have water and forest around me. A fresh water stream perhaps and hopefully a healthy forest. I know places like this and when it is time to move, this is where I will go. I have no specifics on anything that may occur, I only have the perceptions I have gained from being as connected to myself as I am. I was starting to see Teotihuan's point. I gathered all my information from what I felt and I could not feel that without my body. I used my body as a mapping tool to determine, sometimes location and sometimes intensity. It was all making much more sense now. The key would be, how to train myself and help others train themselves to become this sensory tool he was talking about.

I was exhausted, felt like I could sleep for a week. I had a lot going on in my body and was never sure exactly where any specific thing was coming from. I was hoping that this conversation with Teotihuan could possibly clear some things up for me. So I returned to his world, not so much with questions but looking for reasons so many of us felt like our worlds were dissolving right before our eyes. I really felt like many of us were not desperately grasping trying to keep things the same, but rather we were looking for a set of oars, hoping to try and navigate the crazy waters we had been thrown into. As I sit writing this, I look down the bed at my dogs. Even they don't seem to have any energy today. The energy here is very heavy, sleepy energy, which is rather odd for summer. I could feel all kinds of changes taking place but there was no physical proof. Faith, Trust and Patience had become constant companions in the last few months, they were the energy that propelled me forward.

"How are your ears? Yes I am very aware of how exhausted you are. That exhaustion may continue for awhile. You will have days with boundless energy and then for many days following you will have a hard time dragging yourself from your sheets. There are many reasons for this. The main reason is that your spin is starting to

95

separate from the Earth's spin. There are many individual's at this time that are moving away from the polarity. People, just as the planet, had to be polarized to experience 3rd dimensional reality. Now however there are certain individual's that are slightly ahead of the curve and are pulling away from polarity just ahead of the earth doing so. The effectively has a similar action as trying to fight gravity. It is very difficult, and will exhaust you. The Earth's poles have already shifted. That initiated the shift in polarity. However this is not a simple reversal of the poles as most people think, it is a merging of the polarity and that creates a very different effect. Most of these effects will have physical ramifications in not only human bodies, but the bodies of all other species on the planet. You may experience melancholy, time shifting, vertigo, inner ear pressure problems, heart palpitations, sudden loss of memory only to regain it moments later. Other symptoms can be sudden and severe pain that disappears as quickly as it came. Seeing things that disappear the instant you realize you are seeing them. Sudden knowing is also a symptom of this. As the spin changes the network that holds our memories intact, you may in moments be thrown into another life with a different set of talents and you may be able to retrieve the memory of those talents. You may hear voices and then they disappear. One thing that is very recognizable is the feeling that you have just been shocked with electricity. It is momentary, but almost violent. Something else that could happen is you may develop symptoms of some disease but no matter how many tests you take there is not proof of a disease. There is also a feeling of pressure or being watched. There will be moments when if you have the gift of seeing beyond the veil, then you may easily look into other worlds and then they disappear."

"What is occurring is this, Earth has two rates of spin. There is the inner core that spins at a very high rate of speed and an outer skin that spins much slower. That inner core causes the the earth to rotate. However what is happening now is the inner core is slowing down. To be able to raise the vibration of Earth the core needs to change its pace. So the skin on the surface of Earth is going on momentum and is starting to slow a little. The rate of spin of the core and the rate of spin on the surface is no longer synchronized. It is necessary for this to happen to allow the grid to slip. However it is causing many problems in your individually polarized fields as well. Your rate of spin internally is not matching your rate of spin externally. What is on the inside is coming to the surface and you cannot stop it. In some ways it will make time run backwards for you. You may have many thoughts that lead from your present moment to your childhood. Focusing on the future will be difficult until you learn to align the knowing you had as a child with your life purpose."

"Perhaps the easiest way to think of it is this, your insides are turning one way and your outsides are turning another. That is not literal of course, but that is the way it feels. Everything is getting very disjointed, and you are having a very hard time getting your life to make sense based on the standards you have always lived by. Does this help you to understand what is going on?" Teotihuan compassionately offered this. And even though I could understand what he was saying and yes, it did makes sense, it did not help the way I felt.

The roaring in my ears from the blood flowing through them was all consuming. The quieter I was the worse it would get. There was constant pressure and constant sound, rather like standing on the sidelines as a thousand motorcycles pass on the road. A constant roar. My bones were snapping and cracking and I felt like I was dissociating from myself. I knew that would not help, so I tried to crawl deeper into the noise in my head, attach myself to my body in a way that I was not looking through my eyes but feeling through my senses. That helped a little, there was not so much pressure in my head then. It also didn't help that I was on the west coast at the Pacific's edge, the body of water that was to produce a new land mass as the 5th dimension emerged. I had noticed a distinct shift in the energy here in the last 3 months. It was heavier almost felt confused. The light had changed as well. When the sun was out now, I felt as though I was under fluorescent lighting, not natural sunlight. It was a very unusual feeling. I am a lover of soft pink and orange toned light which occurs in other spots on the planet, here though the sunlight made the green leaves look grey. Definitely not what I was used to.

"Yes, moving deeper into your body will help. This is not the same as grounding. You have to find that place inside yourself where you are your own ground. There is a place just below the navel where many people find this spot. It is the place that returns you to the mother, it returns you home, you connection to the divine source. That is the grounding that you are looking for. The way to ground now, is to ground to the source, that place within you that is infinite. You can still ground to the Earth if you wish but you may not get consistent results. Earth is going through her own transition and often will be releasing outward, in those times it will create a reverse energy and grounding to her will be very challenging. Remember the polarities are not reversing, they are merging. Think about what that means in your own body. How do you perceive this will happen in your own body? The time to look inward for answers has come. If you look outward, what you see may deceive you, truth is found within."

"In all of us there is what you would think of as a Black Hole that connects us with the source energy. In your reality only a few have explored those connections. You are coming to a time now that all must discover what that connection is for them. It is the path that leads to what you call teleportation. It is the path that leads to the upper worlds. It is how you discover the whole of who you are, and the time is quickly approaching that you shall see how you are connected to the Earth through this point, and from that spot you are connected to time itself. You have now entered the time of accelerated understanding. You will have moments where you will question your sanity, try not to analyze the moment or you may get stuck in it. You will shift in time both forward and backwards now. It will only last an instant here or there but what you see will be real. Your reality is very porous now, like a sponge. From a distance it looks solid, but it is full of holes. Learn to trust what you feel, what your knowing tells you, because what your eyes see can be easily deceived. Your brain is just a tool that registers and organizes input. It works in a certain way based on physical stimuli. Your mind however is what you use to think. If you trust how the brain organizes information and do not analyze that information with the mind and your knowing, your reality will no longer be your reality. Bare this in mind every time you say to yourself, I can't believe that is true. Truth is the illusion now. All things are separating in some way, even truth. You will need to find your own way of reorganizing information to create a truth that you can exist within. I know this is all very intense information, but it is information that if not spoken, cannot be acted upon. You will know of what I speak when you experience it. Then you shall discover what your truth is. Go now and rest. You are tired and have absorbed a great deal of information today. Think about what questions you wish to ask and then return. I will be waiting." Teotihuan turned and walked towards the stone houses. He was right. It has been an intense day and I was glad to be released. It would take some time to even formulate questions because I just wasn't sure what impact all this information was going to have on me. I really just wanted to sleep.

I stood looking out the window. The ground was carpeted with Buttercups. Brilliant yellow and vibrating in the sun. I remember how as children we would hold a Buttercup under someone's chin to see it shine yellow against their skin. Buttercups were such a happy flower. I thought about how life had gotten so complicated and how when I start reminiscing, there must be something from that time that I am missing. The utter simplicity of sitting in a field of Buttercups and bathing in that divine yellow light. No agenda, no need to be anywhere but in that moment. I was missing a little of that. I had all this information and spent most of my time trying to figure out what to do with it. Information is great, but unless it is organized and structured somehow, all it is, is a bunch of words put together that allows for a few moments of entertainment. I knew I was supposed to do something with it all, I just was not too sure what. I had taken a few days off from Bonampak and was feeling ready to return. Hoping to get some answers from Teotihuan about why I was recording all of this and what I was supposed to do with it. So I lay down and let my self drift through the veil.

"Ah there you are, I was beginning to wonder if you would come back?" Teotihuan came forward and warmly hugged me. He knew this was all getting to me a little.

"Of course I would come back. Even after all this time I still feel like you have all the answers and I have all the questions!" I laughed, realizing I was agitated when I arrived but immediately felt relieved of my burdens when Teotihuan hugged me.

"Are you ready to go on now?" His warm friendly smile was so different from the intensity he exuded last time I was here.

"I am ready when you are" Not that I really was ready, I just didn't know what else to say.

"Ok then, lets get to it. I have felt your questions of late. You wonder what of your life and your calling? You wonder where you are going and if you will ever get there? You wonder why it has all happened this way and will it ever be different? You offer as much as you can to others and yet you still feel a little vacant. You question your own knowing because in the past you thought you knew and it never came to fruition. Your life is one big question mark. However something lately has offered a spark in you, hasn't it? There is something that has been with you since you were born and even though you wonder why, you know why. Is this not true?" Teotihuan was gently nudging me. I was not sure that I knew what he was talking about. I looked at him with a slightly puzzled look. You know that look when you are trying to make your face look questioning but down deep you know that you know the answer so your face just really ends up looking like a distorted pretzel.

"Well I am not sure what you are trying to communicate with that face but let me say this to open that door to your memory. I think it went something like this, when you close your eyes and set yourself free, where do you go?"

Then I knew exactly what he was talking about. A few days ago I had been struggling with the ever present question, "What next?" I can get really obsessive with things. I have a tendency to not be able to leave something alone until I get an answer that feels right to me. Yes I know, sit down get still and the answer is supposed to come, well the amount of times that has worked of me is almost zero. My formula as I am learning in the last couple of years is obsess till you are ready to pull your hair out and then get so frustrated you want beat your head about the wall. Then in the last moment before you do crack your skull, distract yourself with You Tube video's. Well perhaps not just video's but some other form of entertainment, just to get out of my own head. I know it all sounds a little crazy but it is my process and it gives me a greater rate of success than sitting still.

This very thing happened the other day. Like I said I was obsessing and in that moment of frustration, I cleverly distracted myself with something. I honestly cannot remember if I heard it or read it, but Teotihuan was right, the message was, "Close your eyes and set yourself free, where do you go?" I went the same place I have gone all my life. It is somewhere in time in the British Isles. All I know is it is very rural with lots of hills. It is also by the sea. More than that I cannot say. However for me, I think that my heart lives there. I have never been to the British Isles, although it is top spot on my bucket list. Even as I had these thoughts I could feel myself being carried on the wind, over the fields. My whole body was there, I was in the experience.

"You must come back now. We still have much to do." Teotihuan's voice was gentle, not jarring. I think he knew how present I was in that experience.

"Sorry, I am not sure why that happens like that. I just get carried away. I don't know how it happens either. I have never been there and most of the time I think my imagination is really working well because I don't even know if that place is like that or not." My face felt flush with blood, from the cool Atlantic air rushing against it.

"It is your DNA. You are connected to that area. You have had the memories awaken in you of one of your lives there. However there are many more. Your lineage even today is Irish, you know this. You have dismissed it as a place to live many times, because you think you do not like the cold. However recent experiences have taught you that warm humid climates are not what you are looking for either. So now, the question becomes what is in your DNA that keeps calling you there? Do you want to find out? Are you ready to know? Once those doors are unlocked they cannot be unknown. Think on this for a moment." Teotihuan sat back and waited. He had something in his hands that he was fiddling with, keeping himself politely distracted while let me think.

It is true I did have a very vivid memory of an extremely violent life somewhere on the British Isles. I could see every detail, even the disemboweling I had used as a fortune telling practice. I was a really bad dude in that lifetime and I was not sure I wanted to have more details than I already did. It was one of those lives where you die as violently as you lived, and I remembered it all. But the more I thought about it the more I needed to know what, and why I could never really pull my attention from that area of the world. I had been told many times I was under the guardianship of the White Stag, and I didn't know what that meant either. So I decided yes. I needed to know.

"Yes, I want to know. Maybe if I can understand why this connection to that land is so strong I can let it go. Maybe it will unlock something else I need to see so that I can better manage this life I live now. I do feel that it is all connected, I am just not sure how or why. Will you help me?" I found myself speaking with incredible passion verging on the edge of tears. I wanted to either be there for real or find out why I needed to be there. I have been searching for home since the day I was born. Yes I know home lives inside of you and you should be able to create a home anywhere if you are at home in your heart. But something just wouldn't let me quite find that comfort. I needed this.

"Alright. This is a good decision. Now I want you to meet two people that will be able to help you as well."

Coming up the field in that moment were two very tall people. They stood out against most of Teotihuan's people who were generally shorter in height. They were dressed very elaborately. Around their shoulders were coverings of fur, precious stones and some kind of leaves. Around there head were some kind of fabric bindings. Their hair was long. A man and a woman. The woman had long red hair down to her waist and the man was fair haired, the colour of wheat after it dries in the sun. They both stood more than six feet tall. They were close now and I could feel the energy emanating from them. Their stature was imposing, but I felt no threat from them.

They stood directly in front of me now, smiling gently. I had to look up to meet their eyes. I felt that they knew me, but I could not recall them. Teotihuan introduced the woman as Faedrae and the man as Guiliam. They removed their cloaks as I am sure the heat was getting to them. Against their skin they wore long tunics of white. The fabric seemed to be made of a soft cotton and was decorated in symbols. The belts were knotted and made of what looked to be natural fibre as well. Light came from them, they seemed to glow. They reached out and offered me their hand in greeting.

"It has been a long time. We are happy to see you again. We were not sure we ever would. I know this is confusing, we know you and you do not think you know us, but you will remember, and many of your questions will be answered then. We are at your service. Call upon us at any time. Much will change soon and we are happy to shed light where there may be dark. Use your voice, take it to the world, the answers will come." Guiliam placed his hand on one shoulder and Faedrae placed her hand on the other. When they did that I felt very safe, even though I was struggling with my confusion. Then they picked up their cloaks, turned and left. They did not look back.

"What was that all about? Where did they come from? They do not belong here. Who are they?" I looked at Teotihuan who seemed to have a very bemused look on his face. I was standing half bent over with my hands spread out at the sides of my body, and my eyes popped wide open. It must have looked pretty funny cause all the Toltecs were laughing pretty hard.

"You will find out soon enough who they are. I will tell you that they hold the answers to your DNA connection to the British Isles.

Over the next short time, much will come to light. Do not be afraid to speak with them the same way you speak to me. They are waiting for you, however they do understand we must finish our business first" A loud clap came from the palms of Teotihuan. I guess he was not too sure how present I was. I blinked my eyes and then squinted them. I had heard what he said but seemed incapable of a response. I had a love hate relationship with change, and he knew it was usually best to spring things on me in the moment to avoid my avoidance. However I was still a little shocked at the moment. So I sat down on the lawn and gently rolled back onto my spine, listening to every snap and crack as I did.

"Hmmmm, interesting", was all I could muster. I just had no words.

"Now back to what to do with all this information. Like Guiliam said, you must take it to the world. However you may wish to organize it in a way that the information can be absorbed as knowledge. Often people are not sure what to do with large amounts of information, so if it is organized, it can become wisdom. You understand this?" Teotihuan was looking to see if I was registering anything he was saying. I was there though and oddly present.

"Yes I do understand exactly what you mean. It is the difference between whether or not someone can absorb what they are reading or experiencing. If you can organize it in a way that people learn in layers then it will be much more effective. Right?" Now I felt like smiling.

"Right!" Now Teotihuan was smiling. "So now I am going to offer you a new way to ground yourself, because the old way even though it may still work for you, it will not take you where you may want to go. You can use this whenever grounding to the Great Mother does not work. You can also use this if there is something or somewhere in particular you wish to ground your energy to, or draw energy from. But always be careful that you know what it is you are drawing towards you.

Calm and centre yourself. Allow yourself to relax. Breathe deeply. Close your eyes. Now I want you to form an image in your mind of what you think it would look like if you had a spot in your body where you anchored yourself. The image could be anything as long as it represents security, solidity and safety to you. Once your body is relaxed and you feel calm and present, allow your awareness to slowly move down through your body. In all of us there is a point where we anchor ourselves into our physical bodies. As you move your awareness down through your body pay attention to how it feels. Where you are warm and where you are cold. What parts are easy to move through and what parts are challenging. Move down through your body from one end to another. Now go back to where you started and set your intention to find the anchor point in your body. Once again bring your awareness to your body and slowly move from one end to the other looking for the image you saw earlier that represented your anchor. When you find the spot that holds your anchor, stop and move into that spot. Take some time and explore this spot. How does it feel to you? Is it hard or soft? Is it warm or cool? What colour is it? Does this spot have a name? How do you feel about this spot? Where is the spot located in your body? Are there any memories attached to this spot? When you are finished exploring this spot, just sit with it and thank it for being the safe anchor that it is. This is the place inside of you that you can retreat to if you need to feel safe. This is where you are anchored into your body. It is also the spot you can launch yourself from to anchor yourself in other places. Look at your anchor now. If you look very closely you will see a small door that opens. Inside this door is the method to attach yourself to another spot. It could be a rope, roots or a bungee cord, but whatever it is, it will open a pathway to another place for you to anchor your energy. Now think of somewhere you would like to anchor yourself, perhaps a star or the moon, or maybe the source energy itself. Get a clear image in your mind of what your destination is then remove your line of energy from its container. Now with your intention firmly in mind take the line of energy and throw it will all your might watching it land and anchor itself at its intended destination. As soon as it is anchored it starts to send energy to you. You can feel the energy coming to you and filling your body. You can feel yourself getting calmer and stronger. You can feel this loving energy move through every cell allowing you to be solidly in your physical body. You are present, your are calm, you are congruent. Allow yourself to become completely grounded by this new energy. Once you are full, allow the line of energy between you and your destination to retract itself back into the anchor in your body. Close the door on the anchor and allow yourself to expand your awareness through your whole body once again. As you do this you may want to offers thanks for the new energy. You may want to feel gratitude and marvel at how miraculous the universe is. And now say thank you to yourself for all that you do and all that you have to offer. As you send love outward also send it inward. As you are ready open your eyes.

Chapter Ten

Again I found myself taking a couple days off from joining Teotihuan for lessons. I wasn't tired or even that busy, I was avoiding. I could feel the distancing starting to happen. I knew that my intense lessons with him were coming to an end. So in my mind if I didn't go back, it would drag out my departure. I really liked going there and learning, and I did not want to leave. However I was learning that in my life, nothing ever seemed to be permanent. I was to go somewhere, learn at an intense rate of speed and then go somewhere else to learn a different lesson. I could appreciate the fact that I was never bored for too long, but I often thought that training under the same master for many years would have its advantages. I knew that the people I had just been introduced to were going to be a sort of return in my life. I was not sure what I was returning to and I did not really relish the thought of rehashing the past life memory that they represented to me, but somehow I knew it was inevitable.

I had avoided long enough and I knew I had to return, I wanted to return, I just didn't want to face another ending. So many endings in my life. Yes they always led to new beginnings but the constant change over was starting to make me a little dizzy. Teotihuan was right, I was looking for home. It is something I had been looking for since I was born. I did not feel any closer to finding it now than I did then. Every where I moved, turned out not to be the right place as the energy just seemed to run out after a couple of years. Awhile back I had been offered a vision that told me I was to write a collection of what I thought were chapters for a larger book. What I was discovering is that I was writing a collection of short books, and I was not sure where it all led. It felt like I was writing about significant moments of change in history, and I was hoping it would all add up in the end. Trust and faith were my guides. I knew I was learning a lot through this process, all I could hope was that the people that read these words were learning something as well. So with one last look outside at the butterflies flitting about on the Buttercups, I closed my eyes and let my consciousness walk me through the veil to Bonampak.

As the giant stone table came into view, I could see life as normal. People were milling about and there was a group sitting on the lawn in deep discussion about something. One thing I did not see was Teotihuan. I walked around for a bit, expecting that he was off doing something somewhere, but when I had been there longer than I thought I should be and he still wasn't there I decided to ask around. I asked a couple of people but they had not seen him. Then I saw one of his students, he told me that Teotihuan had gone on a journey to the mountain. I asked what for and he said that he did not know. He just told me that at some point all the masters go to the mountain for guidance. There was no way of knowing when they would be back, he suspected even the masters did not know how long they would be gone. I asked how I could get there. He told me that I can only get there if the master wants me to come. He gave me instructions of what to do and so I set off to do them.

I was surprised that Teotihuan did not tell me not to come back. Something did not feel right to me, but then again I was not familiar with the ways of this dimension. I really had nothing to compare it too. So I settled myself by the great stone table and tried to meditate. I followed my own process of anchoring myself somewhere else. This time I was anchoring myself to Teotihuan in hope that he would pull me in and at least tell me what was going on. I didn't need to stay with him, but some clarification was, in my consideration, only proper manners. I didn't have long to wait as I could feel myself being pulled along my line of energy to where he was.

I was standing on a very narrow path that was being crushed by the dense bush that surrounded it. I could see there was a small opening a few feet ahead, I assumed that is where I would find Teotihuan. As I set myself free from the encumbering darkness of the jungle I could see I was on narrow cliff ledge over looking a beautiful valley where a powerful river snaked across the landscape. The rocky ledge was only a few feet wide, and to fall here would mean certain impalement on the trees below. I could not see Teotihuan, he was not here, so I followed the path in the only direction it led. Along the edge of the escarpment to a small cave. If the path had not led directly there, I would not have seen it. The entrance was small and I had to get down on my hands and knees and crawl in. Inside however the ceiling was high and it was well lit with the powder mixture I had been shown earlier. Two blankets were laid out and I knew then that Teotihuan was expecting me. A slight noise drew my attention to another small opening on the other side of the cave and from it Teotihuan emerged looking happy and rested.

"It took you long enough to get here." He laughed as he spoke. He seemed in such good spirits, like this place was a tonic for him.

"Well no one gave me a map and the GPS wasn't working." I quipped, not stopping to think if he would know what GPS was or not. He just laughed at me and motioned for me to sit.

"Would you like some water? The water here is very good, very pure. It comes up through the mountain from the vast wells below. Some say it is the blood of the mountain and that to drink it will give the life of the mountain to you."

"Well yes in that case I will have some." As I tasted the water, I could feel an energy move through me. I could feel the mountains voice inside of me seeking to know me. It was like the ghost of the mountain merged with me and awoke my memories. I felt myself falling backwards very quickly. I could not say if I was falling upwards or downwards, all I knew was I was moving through time in a reverse manner. I felt a little dizzy and then the motion stopped. Teotihuan was still there with me as I opened my eyes.

"The mountain saw fit to take you on a journey. You have been gone for some time. Did you see anything?" Teotihuans gaze upon me was intense, like he was looking for some kind of sign that it was still me.

"I thought I was only gone for a few moments. That is all it felt like. I did not see anything but darkness. I felt dizzy as I fell, but I did not know what direction I was falling in. Is that the way it is supposed to be?" I had learned not to panic by this point but most of this stuff still did not make sense to me.

"There is no normal now. You have been reset by the mountain. I had a feeling this was going to occur for you, that is why I came to this place, so that you would follow me. I know how you hate having loose ends." His laughter echoed through the cavern and reverberated in the next chamber.

"Reset me? I don't know what that is supposed to mean. Does it have a meaning?" I could feel panic starting now because of his use of terms that had no point of reference for me.

"How you are reset is a very difficult thing to describe, because you don't know how you are reset until a few years down the road. What it really means is that part of your memory has been wiped clean. I do not mean the memory you use everyday to know who you are.

You will still look in the mirror and recognize yourself. What I mean is deeper than that. Much of our memories of how we are supposed to experience life is based on who we have been in other lives. So when you come to this life to learn a certain structure, certain rules about the way things work have to be set up so you can learn what you need to learn in a specific way to get the greatest benefit from it. That structure that is set up is based on the structure of reality when you were here before and set yourself up for this lifetime. So you are born into a similar structure this lifetime that was present in the lifetime where you created the problem that you have now come here to solve. Are you with me so far?" He could probably see that I was still recovering from however long I was gone in the hands of the mountain.

"Ya, I think I have it. Same structure, different times." I just kept nodding my head, that seemed easier.

"Right the time and technology do not matter, the structure of the reality does however. Time and technology are really just props on the stage. The structure of reality is the stage itself. Never confuse the two. Because you are able to create something, does not mean it will change your nature. So when the mountain resets you, it means you have completed part of your journey to the point that you no longer need to be bound to certain structures. So that part of yourself that has those structures imprinted is erased. So the rules of that structure no longer bind you either. Now the fact you did not see anything as you were being reset tells me that the structure you are now moving into is not one of conformity. That is why there is not way to tell you exactly what to expect. There will be a structure in place but it may be so fluid that you are required to make the rules up as you go. However the one thing I can tell you is this new structure is attached to your meeting Guiliam and Faedrae." Teotihuan was being as straight forward as possible. So I would oblige with the same.

"Yes I pretty much already had that figured out. I know that you were passing me off to them and that is the next direction to directly influence my life. Not sure what to do with it though. That is not a pretty lifetime to remember." I could feel a little agitation arising in me.

"Well to be honest it was a bit of a surprise for me as well. They arrived somewhat unexpectedly looking for you and in truth I think you may have known more about it than I. However you are in good hands with them. They are ancient and very good at what they do." I could tell he was trying to talk without saying anything now.

"So what is it that they do?" If he was going to play politician then so was I.

"Well I think you know that is not for me to say, it is for you to experience. After all, would you have come here if you had been told in advance what was up? You know your life is going to happen in a sequence now, you are not stupid, even if you play it that way. You are fulfilling your Bucket List so to speak, and this is the path you have chosen,so?" He nodded his head to me and I wasn't sure if he was offering me compassion or sympathy, but it did worry me a little. An unknown structure through sequencing of lives. That felt like a recipe for disaster to me. Now I was wishing I wasn't so nosey and I hadn't come to the mountain. But what is done is done, now it was just to deal with it.

"You know our time is almost done. Much is about to change. It is the way it is supposed to be and all is in order. It is now that you will discover what the whispers from eight rooms means. It is the last process I will offer you. Take these processes to the people. It has the power to help many. I am here and always will be here. You will never be rid of me. However the direction you thought you were going in when you met me, has now changed. You feel that change because it carries you like the great ocean currents that carry information from one side of the world to the other. The world around you is your teacher and your guide. It is time to use all that I have taught you and take it with you to the next section of your life, where you will learn more. You may return to the mountain again in this life. Never be afraid, because the mountain offers life. All you need to do is accept it. Now go back to your home and your dogs. I will send the process to you. You may see fit to change things to best suit your reality, as long as the structure stays intact the method does not matter. The next time you see me, we shall be back on the great lawn." Teotihuan gave me his instructions and with a wave of his hand the walls of the cave disappeared and I open my eyes to dog drool and a wagging tail that needed to go for a pee. No matter what I had gone through or how magical my life may seem, my dogs always forced me to keep it real.

Find a comfortable spot. Release your body to the support that is beneath it. Breathe deeply and rhythmically. In and out, in and out, till you can feel yourself relax. Relax all parts of your body. Make sure you will not be disturbed and continue breathing deeply. Allow yourself to start feeling distant from your body. Allow yourself to know that your are ready to know more. Close your eyes and breath deeply. Follow the gentle rhythm of your breath, in and out, in and out. Now you are totally relaxed and feeling like you are floating gently just above your body. You are still very connected to your body but not confined by it. Continue to breathe deeply. Now as you are in a state of complete relaxation, give yourself permission to have full knowing of your eight rooms.

The first room of your life is your room of survival. Gently hold the idea of survival in your mind and move through your body. Allow yourself to find the spot where your survival is located in your body. When you find it, look at it very carefully. What does it look like? Is there anyone in that room? Who is it? What colour is the room? How big is it? Is it clean or messy? Can you see yourself in that room? Does something appear to be missing in the room? If so, what? On the other side of the room is a window, open it and look out, you will see what you need for your survival. When you have finished exploring your room of survival, allow yourself to heal whatever may need healing in that room, and when you are finished send love to the room and and bring your consciousness back to the centre.

The second room of your life is connections. Gently hold the idea of connections in your mind and allow your consciousness to move through your body and find this room. Allow yourself to find the spot where your connections is located in your body. When you find it, look at it very carefully. What does it look like? Is there anyone in that room? Who is it? What colour is the room? How big is it? Is it clean or messy? Can you see yourself in that room? Does something appear to be missing in the room? If so, what? On the other side of the room is a window, open it and look out, you will see what you need for your connections. When you have finished exploring your room of connections, allow yourself to heal whatever may need healing in that room, and when you are finished send love to the room and and bring your consciousness back to the center.

The third room of your life is your power. Gently hold the idea of power in your mind and allow your consciousness to move through your body and find this room. Allow yourself to find the spot where your connections is located in your body. When you find it, look at it very carefully. What does it look like? Is there anyone in that room? Who is it? What colour is the room? How big is it? Is it clean or messy? Can you see yourself in that room? Does something appear to be missing in the room? If so, what? On the other side of the room is a window, open it and look out, you will see what you need for your power. When you have finished exploring your room of power, allow yourself to heal whatever may need healing in that room, and when you are finished send love to the room and and bring your consciousness back to the centre.

The fourth room of you life is your love. Gently hold the idea of love in your mind and allow your consciousness to move through your body and find this room. Allow yourself to find the spot where your connections is located in your body. When you find it, look at it very carefully. What does it look like? Is there anyone in that room? Who is it? What colour is the room? How big is it? Is it clean or messy? Can you see yourself in that room? Does something appear to be missing in the room? If so, what? On the other side of the room is a window, open it and look out, you will see what you need for love. When you have finished exploring your room of power, allow yourself to heal whatever may need healing in that room, and when you are finished send love to the room and and bring your consciousness back to the centre.

The fifth room of your life is your truth. Gently hold the idea of truth in your mind and allow your consciousness to move through your body and find this room. Allow yourself to find the spot where your connections is located in your body. When you find it, look at it very carefully. What does it look like? Is there anyone in that room? Who is it? What colour is the room? How big is it? Is it clean or messy? Can you see yourself in that room? Does something appear to be missing in the room? If so, what? On the other side of the room is a window, open it and look out, you will see what you need for truth. When you have finished exploring your room of power, allow yourself to heal whatever may need healing in that room, and when you are finished send love to the room and and bring your consciousness back to the centre.

The sixth room of your life is your perception. Gently hold the idea of perception in your mind and allow your consciousness to move through your body and find this room. Allow yourself to find the spot where your connections is located in your body. When you find it, look at it very carefully. What does it look like? Is there anyone in that room? Who is it? What colour is the room? How big is it? Is it clean or messy? Can you see yourself in that room? Does something appear to be missing in the room? If so, what? On the other side of the room is a window, open it and look out, you will see what you need for perception. When you have finished exploring your room of power, allow yourself to heal whatever may need healing in that room, and when you are finished send love to the room and and bring your consciousness back to the center.

The seventh room of your life is your reception. Gently hold the idea of reception in your mind and allow your consciousness to move through your body and find this room. Allow yourself to find the spot where your connections is located in your body. When you find it, look at it very carefully. What does it look like? Is there anyone in that room? Who is it? What colour is the room? How big is it? Is it clean or messy? Can you see yourself in that room? Does something appear to be missing in the room? If so, what? On the other side of the room is a window, open it and look out, you will see what you need for reception. When you have finished exploring your room of power, allow yourself to heal whatever may need healing in that room, and when you are finished send love to the room and and bring your consciousness back to the centre.

The eighth room of your life is your Oneself. Gently hold the idea of the Oneself in your mind and allow your consciousness to move through your body and find this room. Allow yourself to find the spot where your connections is located in your body. When you find it, look at it very carefully. What does it look like? Is there anyone in that room? Who is it? What colour is the room? How big is it? Is it clean or messy? Can you see yourself in that room? Does something appear to be missing in the room? If so, what? On the other side of the room is a window, open it and look out, you will see what you need for the Oneself. When you have finished exploring your room of power, allow yourself to heal whatever may need healing in that room, and when you are finished send love to the room and and bring your consciousness back to the centre.

Now allow yourself to remember all the details you need to know to make positive changes in your life. Slowly allow yourself to become aware of your body. You are light and happy and when you are ready, open your eyes.

Chapter Eleven

I was far too aware that my time with Teotihuan was coming to an end. I was not sure how many more times I would get to be there with him in the position as student. I was stressing about what it was I really wanted to know about his reality. Because of not knowing how much time was left, I really wanted to make the most of it. I was trying to think of exactly how I could ask some questions to get the most out of the information. Yes I wanted to ask personal questions but more than that I wanted to ask, what was the 5th really like in comparison to the 3rd. I knew already that he would only answer certain questions about me personally. I was never sure if that was because he did not know or that he was not allowed to interfere. So I decided to keep my questions more general. What would I want to know if I was interviewing him? This was the best position for me to take. Once this was decided, it seemed easier to formulate questions in my mind, and i felt a little more comfortable with what would turn out to be my last visit in this way.

I lay down repeating my questions over and over again in my mind, hoping that I would not forget them. As I closed my eyes I could feel myself travelling through the darkness in a direction I never knew, drifting across time till my feet were touching solid ground again.

I could hear the buzz of the people as I opened my eyes. I was on the great lawn near the stone table. The energy was high as everyone was busier than normal. They seemed to be harvesting different food stuffs and were doing it in such a joyful manner. I scanned the many white tunics looking for Teotihuan, he was standing by a group of women, seemingly in lively discussion about something. The second I found him with my eyes he seemed to know I was there, as he turned his head to look at me. He smiled and made a few hand gestures to the ladies and started making his way towards me. There seemed to be so many more people going about their day than I was used to.

"Ah my friend, welcome back. Today for the first time you get to see what life here is like on a daily basis. There is always much to do, and many happy faces to do it. How are you?" Teotihuan was really greeting me like someone from a neighbouring town that he hadn't seen for awhile. I was delighted by this, he seemed to be in such a great mood.

"Well I am good, but I have splintered emotions. I know we are coming to an end with our sessions and I am not really wanting that to happen. So I am happy to see you and sad that I am not sure how much longer I will be seeing you?" I was being honest. That was the only way to be with him.

"All of life is a cycle. If one thing did not end another could not begin and there would be no growth. You can get very stuck in wanting things to go on past their natural ending, and that grasping is not healthy for you or the thing you are grasping to. I know you understand this but you must practice it more. The ideal life would be to know when things must start and when they must end. If you could do this you would have the greatest amount of energy involved in any experience you have. The greatest amount of impact on your reality, and it would not dissipate or mutate into something you did not desire, by grasping. Yes?" I knew he was exactly right. When I like something I want it to continue instead of honouring the moments that I've already had, I try to find ways to make it last longer than its natural time. He is right, he is always right.

"If it is alright I would like to interview you and ask you some questions about life here. I think it would be the best way to make the most of the time we have spent together. Some of the things you have shown me make sense but still I have a hard time really understanding the technology of it. So I would just like to have a conversation that makes sense to me, something that I can take home and really use as a tool. If you don't mind?" That was truly what I wanted. Something I could keep with me almost as a memento of the time I had spent there.

"That is a stupendous idea. I am most delighted you thought of it. Splendid, lets get to it then shall we." It was funny but he was suddenly speaking very differently than I was accustomed to. Almost British I thought. I had to laugh as we went to find a quiet spot on the lawn. It was so busy that day it was hard to find a little area where we could create a bubble of silence.

"Wow, I am not used to it being like this. So busy, I am finding it hard to concentrate." I was feeling very distracted by the amount of life that was happening.

"Life is a good thing. It is usually like this here, it is just that you have been shielded from the intensity of it so you could get the education you needed. The trick to life is to create a bubble with a solid but flexible boundary. Life is something that you need to participate in. However you also need solitude to have balance. You need to be able to create your own individual bubble within the business of life. You do not want the boundaries of that bubble to be so solid that life can't get in and you can't get out, but you do want it to be strong enough to define the space you need to be in at any given moment. Boundaries should be made with the energy of water. If something hits the surface of water with great speed it will bounce right off as though the water is repelling it. However if something approaches the surface carefully and cautiously with respect, water will yield and entrance will be granted. So your boundaries should be like that. Flexible enough to encompass the energy that approaches with respect, but strong enough to repel that which approaches from an attack position. You understand this?" Teotihuan face, almost seemed to change a little. I could tell he was in wisdom mode now. Every thing he said to me at this time was going to be layered. The same sentence would have many meaning depending on how I heard what I heard. This way I can literally take this information home and every time I refer to it, I will hear it in a different way. I was very happy about this, because it was exactly what I was looking for.

"Yes I understand this very well. Far too often I make my boundaries of earth or air, and it does not work very well. One is too hard to move and the other offers very little resistance. I will take that advice gratefully. Thank you. Now may I ask some more questions?" I was feeling most affected by his energy now, like I was floating but still tethered to the ground.

"Of course, that is what we are here to do." He smiled a beautiful smile and my heart opened.

"Ok, what would I like to know? I think I would like to know how it is you see us in our reality?" I knew that was a rather loaded question, but I had thought it might just help to see myself from another perspective.

Teotihuan started to laugh, so I knew he would be lighthearted in his response. "How do we see you? Well, we have been you, so our perspective is not limited to judgement. We have had the experience you are having now so our perception of you starts with compassion. Even though we exist in a different space, we are directly connected

117

to your reality and therefore we do experience the bleed through from your world as a mass consciousness experience. For the most part, veils between realities is rather porous so there are places in our world where we can see clearly into your reality. It is the same in your world, you can see clearly into other realities as well. The times you are in right now are very stressful. I remember all too well how much our world changed in such a short time before we crossed over into this world. In the span of a lifetime, our world became unrecognizable to us. The same thing is happening to you now. You are being asked to expand your perception so quickly that everything feels like it is popping open every where. All of you are seeking safety in some form. It is essential that you decide what safety is for you so that you can seek it appropriately. All of your people are being driven by primal fear and movement has become non stop even if you are standing still. When you finally do manage to be still it feels like such an unnatural thing, you start moving again. It is almost painful to be still at this point, however it is exactly what you need. So many are looking for distraction of any kind because the intensity of the false self has become unbearable for them. Here is what is happening as plainly as I can say it. The momentum of all the lives you have lived on your current time line is flowing with purpose now. Like a giant river of learning, lessons and karma the river has come to the damn, which is you. All that energy is pushing against you right now. The irresistible force has met the immoveable object. So what do you do now? Whatever you have not dealt with from a karmic perspective is going to become the dragon of fear in your life. You need to be still enough to discover what these lessons are and deal with them. You will always find your lessons when you look to the area's of your life that have not been working for a long time. Please do not misunderstand me. It is not that you have to clear this karma to ascend, you can bring it with you, however if you do, it will be even more amplified here. So dealing with your suffering now, will bring great advantages to the control you have when you cross over. So to really answer your question, I have great empathy for what you are going through. I wish you would all turn to one another and offer whatever help you can in the way of doing what you do to your highest ability. It is a time to find unity now, not dispersion. The raging karmic river that runs within you is easier to manage when you offer your understanding to all others that are experiencing the same intensity."

"I like the metaphor of the karmic river that actually helps me a lot. That is how it feels in my life. There is an incredible pressure and immediacy to everything that happens now. It all feels like, if I don't get this done in this second, I will die! It is hard to deal with that. Do you have any advice on how to deal with that intensity?" I think my exhaustion was showing when I asked that question. I knew many people who were dealing with that feeling of holding back a river, and trying to act as though nothing was wrong.

"My best advice would be to get honest about it. That is the first step. So many people in your society see it as weakness if they do not feel that they are perceived as super human. They feel inadequate when they cannot do it all. What I hope to convey now is that you need to understand you are not supposed to do it all. That is not what life is about. That is not sharing, it is being selfish. It seems as though most people in your society would like to have a different economic structure. However the mentality is not there to support it. To have a structure where people feel accepted for who they are and free to pursue their talents, there needs to be no shadows cast upon whatever one chooses to do. There should be no difference between someone who cleans toilets or someone who does heart surgery. In your reality, most that do so called menial labour are looked down upon to the point where they feel disgraced to do their job. How can you create a new economic reality if you allow a caste system to exist? Now to get back to your question. If you were to create a reality where you were able to pursue your passions and allow everyone else to do the same with equal acknowledgement, you would not feel like you had to do it all. You could do the things you were good at and allow others to do what they were good at. This is why I say, trying to do it all is selfish, because you are doing things that you are not very good at and begrudging them, while if you were to let them go, the job could be done much better by someone who would love to do it. Do you see what I am getting at here?" Teotihuan relaxed for a moment waiting for me to assess what he had said and get back to him.

"I think I see what you are saying. You are telling me that we need to change our mind set from thinking we need to do and deal with it all to how much of what I don't want, can I share with someone that wants it. You are telling me that until we start to shift our mindset nothing is really going to change. We have the idea of what sharing really is, backwards. I like your idea but it is not really practical

119

considering we all need money and I know I would love to hand some of my obligations off to others, but I couldn't afford to pay them to do the job. So I like the idea but not sure how it would work in my world?" It was truly a great idea, but I felt down deep that we were too far gone to adopt this system realistically.

"Well you can do as you like in your reality, but when you ascend, this is the reality you will discover. It is not about fully adopting and acting on the method, however it is about adopting the idea. The more you are open to the give and take that life has to offer from this perspective, the more prepared you will be for the actuality of this reality. That is how we manage work load here. Very rarely do you see someone doing something they do not want to do. However all jobs have equal honour, no matter how you would describe them. My job is not different than the person that scrapes the fruit or he that grinds the powder for our light. It is all the same, because it takes all of it to make our society work. You would also benefit greatly from adopting this perspective in your own life. Apply it to all the events that occur to you personally. Instead of perceiving them as good and bad, perceive them as events in your life that allow you the opportunity to grow through different circumstances and variety. Because without experience there is no wisdom. The polarity on your planet is at such an extreme that very few people are able to let go of their attachment to good and bad. They are so attached to a limited emotional experience that they try to eliminate all experiences that do not conform to their preference. What kind of life is that? That is a one dimensional life. When you try to create this kind of reality for yourself you become the dot that lives at the end of the sentence. You are aware of your own presence but you do not embrace the presence of all the other letters that are there. Here in this reality, you have to acknowledge all experiences as equal, because if you react more to one than another, it will directly affect your environment, in whatever way you chose to react. If you cannot control that, your environment can kill you. It is that simple." He smiled and nodded his head and that was all.

"Ok so you are trying to tell me that we are so attached to preference that it actually causes all the chaos in our society. All the energy we exert trying to force life to be the way we want it to be could be much better used by simply allowing life to happen through us and not to us. Or is that a perception to?" I really got this but wanted him to be a little more specific.

"Oh I like, you are catching on to this. Let life happen through you not too you. Yes this is most accurate. Somewhere on your time line you decided that you were supposed to control your life. This is not true. The only control you are supposed to have is how you choose to experience life as it happens. All the energy that you exert outwardly should be applied inwardly, then you would be living according to natural law. Instead of saying, I have to do this, you should say, I must be this. You spend all your time thinking you should become this or that and in truth all you have to do is open the door to allow that which you already are. You do not think of yourself as complete, you think of yourself as deficient, and there is no truth in this. You measure yourself by the people that have what you think you want, but you do not know if those things make them happy. You gamble your energy on an illusion. You would serve yourself much better to spend your energy on what makes you happy, even if that thing changes over time, than you would chasing what you think makes someone else happy. That is a chronic disease in your society right now. People are so afraid to deal with what they will find internally they try to live someone else's life, and that always ends in disaster. I cannot stress strongly enough that this is your life, and you are the only one in it. You were the only one born in it and you will be the only one to die in it, so if you want to own anything of significance, own your life." Teotihuan got up and started moving around. It was like he had a tremendous amount of energy running through him at the moment and movement was the only way he could unleash it.

"I agree with everything you are saying, but we are so staunch in our perspectives, how do we get to that place of running our own lives?" I had heard this so many times from so many different belief systems in my life. It was a basic truth as far as I was concerned, but I was still miles from accomplishing it.

"You must want it. You have to be honest with yourself about how different your life will be if you allow it to become this way. You as a society are addicted to drama, and polarity allows that drama to exist. You must really understand where your focus is. Is it on truly creating peace and balance, or do you actually make decisions that lead you to drama? Do you wait till the last moment to pay your bills? How often does the needle in your car show empty? How often do you give yourself permission to cheat on your diet just so you can put those 5 pounds on, so you can struggle to take them off

121

again? You are so entrenched in drama, you don't identify it as drama. So that is where you start. You need to be aware consistently for a couple of weeks in your life of why you are making the decisions you make. Will this decision bring balance or will it bring drama? There are always going to be those times when a decision will bring drama and it cannot be avoided. This is fine. It is part of learning to allow life to flow through you. All you can do is make as many decisions as possible that will bring balance. When life gets messy then you have the opportunity to practice balance within chaos. That is how you own your life. You don't own your life through avoidance, you own it by masterfully navigating the choppy waters." His answers were pretty direct. I guess so many times in my life I had spent more energy on thinking about what I had to do, than actually doing it.

"Yes, life is a verb, whether you want it to be or not." He added laughing as hard as he could. I actually thought he was going to tip over. I was still unsure if he could hear my thoughts or he was just so well versed in human nature that he knew where my thoughts would go.

"Ok enough about what we need to change. I want to know more about this place. What are the biggest differences between this reality and the one I live in?" I needed a change of pace. I wasn't sure if that was a decision towards balance or chaos and quite frankly I didn't care. I just wanted more understanding of his reality.

"There are many similarities between your reality and here, however they are expressed in a very different way. Lets see, where to start first? As I have mentioned before, the biggest change you notice when you get here is how your energy interacts with the environment. If you are not in control of who you are, then your environment will reflect that. So that took some getting used to. One of the other differences is what we were just talking about. There are no caste systems here. It is essential to happiness here, that you do what you are. There is a drive to master what you choose as well. There is always another level to uncover or another perspective to view things from. So even though you may think we would get bored doing the same thing, we actually progress through many levels of doing it. That is something else that is very different here than in your reality. In your reality there is access to 5 dimensional levels of reality. Here we have access to 8 dimensional levels of reality. We cannot ascend again until we have reached the tipping point for the seventh dimension. At this point we are a good distance from that. We are still flesh and blood people like you, however our energies do flow in different ways. Our physical structures conduct more energy than your bodies do. It is simply that our frequencies are higher and therefore can hold more light. The soul will always be the soul and that never changes, however we are capable of doing certain things you are not. For instance if we were to sit down and have a meal of all the highly processed foods you eat, it would cripple us. It would not only make us critically ill, it would cause a crash in our energetic systems that we may not be able to correct. One of the major differences between your experience of your body and our experience of our bodies is that we are connected to our bodies in a way that we perceive them as our greatest gift. We value and honour our bodies because we know that we live in them for as long as we choose and if we don't maintain them, our reality would consume us. Our bodies are the tools we use to maintain our environments. They are the tools we use to grow in wisdom and knowledge. They are the tools we use to reproduce. We do not in any way take our bodies for granted. They are our greatest prize and we maintain them to extremely high standards. This is what you miss in your quest for longevity." As I looked at him, he seemed to be pulsing. He would fade slightly and then become boldly there, and then fade again. I was not sure if it was my eyes or if he was indeed fading in and out. I also wondered if it had something to do with the topic of conversation. I knew there was no way I would have enough time to get all my questions answered, so I had better press on.

"What do you mean our quest for longevity? Can you elaborate on that?" This is a subject I was interested in. I needed at least 300 years to do most of the learning I felt I needed. If I could expand my chances of being around a little longer, why not?

"Of course. In your reality you mistake your bodies for your permanent home. You use your body to fill all the needs that you do not fill for yourself? Your body is part of you yes, but it is not who you are. You live in your body to have the experiences you need to evolve. The body is an elaborate organic computer, however you mistake it for the amusement park that you cannot escape from. You look to your body and what you can experience through it for your entertainment, your comfort, your communion with god and your feeble attempt at immortality through progeny, but you treat it like a garbage dump. You expect your body to give you all the things in life that you desire, and at the same time you expect it to hide all your secrets. You fill your body with all the emotional garbage you do not want to deal with. You do not feed it to benefit your desire's. You treat it like your worst friend and expect it to never question you or your motives. You will experience reality, in the same way you treat your body. So if you feel like you are always working and no one ever acknowledges you, perhaps you need to stop for a moment and ask yourself if you are treating your body in the same way? Are you constantly filling you body with junk, physically, mentally and emotionally? No matter what you put in your body, it is going to leave a residue. It is up to you to decide if that residue is going to help your body or hurt your body. If you constantly feed your senses with violence, they will become very desensitized to it. Your body will then process pain in a different way than it would if you abhorred violence. Desensitizing yourself to pain can be very dangerous when it comes to alerting yourself to problems within the body. If you were going to put your hand on a hot stove, that prospective pain would process differently than it would in other people. Same with other emotions. If you continue to expect your body to store all your negative emotions, at some point it will hit its tipping point and something somewhere will get clogged beyond its ability to clear itself and a problem will start. It could be cancer or clogged arteries, or even kidney stones. The point is, in your reality you do not perceive your body as a part of you that you are in partnership with. You own your body so you can do anything to it you want, it is your body! Then when your body starts to fail, you feel betrayed like you had nothing to do with it. However if you didn't maintain your car for a long time and it broke down, you would understand, you might be angry but you would still understand."

I had to laugh because he was so very right. I had been guilty of that for a long time. Treating my body as a replaceable possession, not an irreplaceable partner. This was a good education for me. I could see his point. I don't think in our reality we thought so much about the residue that our emotions and our thoughts left. We thought more about the junk that we ate or the alcohol we drank as leaving residue. Now I would think much more about the energetic residue and how we are still continuously damaging ourselves with negative thoughts.

"This is stuff I really needed to hear. So how do we change it? I know our patterns run deep with this way of thinking that our bodies belong to us and we have the right to do what we want to them. How do we shift this?" This is something I really wanted to know.

"Well you have to start thinking more globally. Where does your body come from?" he posed a valid question.

I sat there scratching my head as he patted the ground. At first I just thought he was getting a little impatient, but then I realized he was giving me the answer.

"Our bodies come from the earth." Yes, that was right, we were made of the elements.

"Yes, our bodies come from the earth. Yes we are made of the Great Mother's flesh. So we do not own our bodies, we are just borrowing them. The Great Mother's gift to us is to allow us to use her flesh to create our own, and in this way we are all her children. When we fill our bodies up with garbage be it physical, mental or emotional and then return that body to the Great Mother after we die, it is very much an insult. The mother did not offer us her flesh so that we could give it back to her in worse shape that she gave it to us. Think about that for a moment. Have you ever loaned someone something of yours and they brought it back broken? What did you feel? Insulted? Did you feel like you didn't matter? Did you loan that person more of your stuff? No probably not. But this is not the Great Mother. The Great Mother continues to give us her flesh for our skin suits even though we return them to her in very bad condition. It is because the Great Mother is compassion and healing by her very nature. However it is getting to the point now that her body is getting blocked and clogged and she cannot function in the same way she used to so she must detox, and this is why she is shedding her skin, it will give her a new body to work with. Now I imagine you are still wondering what I meant when I mentioned longevity? Is this is something you would like for me to elaborate on as well?" Teotihuan was being very generous with is time and his wisdom. I was starting to wonder if I might be able to come back once more to finish this.

"Yes please, I would love to know more about longevity and how it can be achieved." I could feel some excitement stir in me. I sat up to be able to hear his words better.

"Longevity is not just a physical thing. It has to be approached holistically if it is to be achieved. On a physical level it is about understanding the partnership between you the energy being and the body that you inhabit. Your body is the gift that allows you to experience this reality in a sensual way. If you respect that and work

125

with your body instead of assuming you know what is best for it, longevity can be accomplished. What this means is you must get to know the skin suit you wear. You must pay close attention to how it reacts to what you put in it. In the physical sense I mean food and drink. It is your job to manage the reactions of your body. If you put too much in your body that brings a negative reaction, then you are not headed towards longevity. Your body is organic this is something you must remember. It is made of the same stuff the earth is made of. That would imply that you should fuel it with pure earth stuffs, however that is not the current practice in your reality.

Exercise is essential to the well being of the body. The body is designed like a pump. If you do not move, it is not able to pump fluid in the manner it needs to. Consistency is the key. Many practices in your reality are to the extreme. Originally the body was designed to connect with Earth's electromagnetic field and balance its polarity in this way, Many cities make this impossible now and people do not realize the importance of this balance. This balance is essential to keeping the field that maintains congruency of thought within the brain, intact. Mental illness is rampant in your reality, for very good reason.

How you live your life will show on your body over time. I said earlier, your body does not lie, so however you are living will become part of your physical body. To much imbalance in your mental body and it will have a great impact on your nervous system. To much imbalance in your emotions, and it will heavily affect your organs and fluids.

Everything in your reality is a mirror of you and what you came here to experience. You body is a mirror, your environment is a mirror, the people around you are mirrors. If you want to understand the full ramifications of all of this, you must be very well anchored in your body and fully aware of it at all times. The way your grow beyond your body is by going through it, not by trying to deny you have a body. It is by being aware of the body and how you are affecting it on all levels that you can pave the way to longevity. Be aware of when the body needs cleaning. The body is designed to allow life to flow through it. It is not designed to be a closet for you to hide everything in. Flow is the bodies theme, as it should be the theme of your experience. Most of the people in your reality have great resistance to flow, and therefore illness and disease rule the day.

The only time this does not apply is when you have chosen an illness or a disability to help you evolve. This can be an effective plan for some. By choosing a physical problem as a process to evolution, it forces you to explore probabilities that you would never normally look at. That or you decide to exit and come back with a different plan. Longevity is based on the balance of all levels of your personal existence and how you manage input and output. It is really that simple. You must also believe that it is possible to live a very long time in a healthy way. Without belief you may as well stuff your face with poison. It has the same effect. Does this satisfy your curiosity about longevity?" He was getting tired. It has been an abnormally long time we had spent together.

"Well not really. I guess I was looking for a step by step, but after what you said, I realize that actually is a step by step if I was to apply it to my life. I can see you are getting tired. May I come back again and talk some more. It just doesn't feel finished to me yet?" I didn't want to sound desperate but I knew all had not been said yet.

"Yes that is fine. You are right there is more you need to know. Come back tomorrow and we will finish it. Safe journeys and sweet blessings!" He rose and left his spot, returning to the rolling mounds that held the temples. I felt he was going to replenish himself. I left and woke up in my bed. Always a little disappointed to be back to normal reality.

Doing as I had been asked, I returned the next day. I felt it was my last formal visit, so I was both happy and sad. Grateful to have had the experience and a little wistful at knowing it was time to move on. The theme in my life was always change, and not subtle change. I never seemed to know exactly where I was going, but was usually delighted when I arrived. This was no different. I had been pulled into this world with no previous knowledge that I was coming here. Initially delighted, then slightly distressed about the adventure, it all worked itself out. Now it was coming to an end. That meant that another adventure would soon start and as curious as I was about that, I was sad to be leaving this place.

I looked across the great lawn. It seemed calmer today. People were going about their business here and there, but it was not the rush that I had encountered yesterday. Teotihuan had seen me and waved. He was just finishing up a conversation. So I wandered over to the spot where we had sat yesterday and plopped myself down to wait. In a moment Teotihuan came rushing towards me waving his arms. I stood up wondering what all the commotion was all about.

"Come, come. I want to show you something we have not talked about here. You will like this." He was almost out of breath he was so excited.

I did as I was told and he led me to a spot in behind the temples. In behind the trees there was a natural arch made in the stone walls that led inside the mountain. In we went and not far inside I could see what he was so excited about. There was some kind of machine that looked like a giant bubble with seating inside. There was seating for four.

"This is how we travel when we have too. It is not often we use the vehicle because we do not have the need, however because this is your last visit, I thought you would like to see something we have not talked about yet. Would you accompany me?" Teotihuan was beaming with excitement.

I looked at the machine again and was very excited at the thought of getting in and going, but in truth, because of my experience with this society that seemed to be so anti technology, I really wondered if Teotihuan was able to drive it. My curiosity however got the best of me.

"Sure lets go!" I enthusiastically offered.

The doors had tiny almost invisible handles on them. We got inside and I realized you could see 360 degrees. Even the floor was see through. From the outside it was easy to see it was a bubble, but from the inside it was actually difficult to see that you were inside of anything. It was a little unnerving as I didn't know how this thing was going to move yet.

We got in and sat in the seats. You could hear the doors seal themselves but I couldn't really see the line where they had sealed. Teotihuan placed a board of lights on his lap and he touched a couple of symbols. When he did this the vehicle seemed to come to life. It was very quiet and all I could hear was a slight hum, and a tiny feeling of tingling on my skin. We lifted straight up into the air through a hole above us that I had not noticed before. We were in the air flying. Teotihuan was talking a mile a minute, but in truth I did not hear much of what he was saying. I was magnetized to the world in front of me. We were flying over the jungle and massive rivers. From up here the world was pulsing with energy that I could not see on the ground. In some areas the ship would seem to shift somehow and Teotihuan would attend to the lights on the board.

"Why do you do that? I can feel the ship change. What is

happening?" I wanted to know we were not going to plunge to the ground.

"This ship runs on energetic output from the planet. There is an elaborate map of portals and vortexes all around us, depending on whether the energy is inputting or outputting and whether it is a portal or a vortex, the ship has to adjust for the type of energy it uses. So as we approach a vortex coming from a portal, the energy source changes and we need to operate in a slightly different mode. This ship is in some ways a living ship that operates within the plasma of earth. The plasma will take on slightly different qualities if a vortex passes through it rather than a portal. Rather like the quality of the wind is different it you are in a desert as opposed to the sea. Are you understanding this?" I could tell Teotihuan loved to fly. I had no idea they had this technology.

"Well I can understand the idea of what you are talking about but I do not understand how this thing flies. I am not the best with technology even in my reality. I do however know that the earth has a huge output of energy, it is just that in my reality we have not really figured out how to harness it yet. I had no idea you had this technology? I honestly didn't think you had anything to do with technology. How did I miss this?" I was a little embarrassed to admit it, but it was true. I had seen absolutely no indication of technology in all my visits to Bonampak.

"We have a great deal of technology in this reality however it differs from your technology in that it all mimics organic technology. Something that was discovered here was that technology in your reality is basically backwards, for going forwards. They kept trying to reinvent the wheel. You would call it ego based technology. Science tried to copy something they saw in the natural world but they tried to recreate it synthetically so they could win whatever prize was popular at the moment. Here technology is approached differently. Nature is our teacher and what we seek to do is honour our teacher as much as possible. So when we have a problem that needs solving, our greatest minds ask for a solution from the Great Mother. She has not let us down yet. Then we work in co operation with her to refine what she has offered in a way that it will organically serve us as well. None of this would have been possible if we had not accepted our bodies as organic computers. When I first came here we were still very attached to our bodies as something that needed to be controlled. Once we able to appreciate our bodies as the vehicle that carried us and allow enough separation to happen so that we could truly understand the wisdom of the body, we started to understand the wisdom of the Great Mother as well. After all we are mirrors of each other. Understanding ourselves allowed us to understand the world around us. This is what is missing in your reality now. I love this flying machine. Now look out there, far ahead in the distance. What do you see?" Teotihuan was straining his neck as though he could see better if he head was further forward. It looked so funny to see him act like a kid I broke out in to laughter.

I did however look forward into the distance and it looked like there was a city there. The jungle thinned and beyond that I could see buildings. They did not look like the buildings I was used to though. And then even further beyond that, I could see the sea. That excited me, the sea was in my blood and it always excited me.

"Ah, yes, that makes sense. You looked beyond the city and to the sea. In our world you would choose to live by the sea in a natural landscape. I wondered where you would choose and that is part of the reason I brought you here. Although to be honest I did not want you to think that our reality was just short brown people in white dresses that lived a primal life in the jungle. Here in this reality we have five different levels of experience that can be lived in any setting.

"So you are telling me that you come here and choose to be stuck in one spot until you learn what you need to learn. What if you have difficulties? What if there is no food? What if you get sick?" I could feel a little panic happening. Why would anyone want to live like that?

"Remember that if you are having problems with food, then you are not monitoring your body in such a way that creates abundance in your environment. In this reality you are consciously in control of your environment. However some lessons are easier to learn in specific settings. It really depends on how you want to design your life. Is this making sense to you?" Teotihuan was still flying around the city, I was getting the feeling he was looking for something.

"I can hear what you are saying but I am not so sure I really understand. You are telling me that if I had lessons to learn around people I may want to live in a city, because there is a higher concentration of people. However if I had lessons to learn about myself I may want to live in the jungle because that way I have to deal with myself directly. Is this right?" I thought I had the general idea. I can say I was not really a big fan of what I was hearing, I guess I felt it limited my freedom.

"That is the basic idea and all you really need to understand right now. However here we have 5 different levels of reality that you can consciously participate in. So this city we are over right now is mid level. It is a living city that is still quite dependent on technology but has incorporated buildings that are like gardens so that they are not dependent on the outside world for food. We have cities that exist in the ocean and cities that are in the ice as well. Each different level is like a world unto itself. A realm of experience that you become totally engulfed in to the point you forget the rest of the worlds exist." The excitement in his voice trailed off a little when he said that.

"I am not so sure I like that idea. How is it you know all about this if one world forgets about another?" I was honestly getting a little confused now.

"Well the forgetting is never complete. Every realm is in contact with all other realms at all times. The elders in each society knows of all realms and we regularly get together to make adjustments as we evolve. There are those of us that choose to stay here and spend lifetimes so we can help this dimension evolve. I have lived in all realms, and my home is still the jungle that I was born to in your reality. This is the way of familiarity. Most, in the end, choose to be in the realm they were born too. It is human nature. And even though you may not think of us as human, we are. We are just slightly more evolved that you." I could feel the genuineness in his voice. He wanted me to know we were the same and that the only thing that really separated us was time and lessons.

"Can we fly over the sea? I just want to see what it is like here. Please?" I was not sure why I so desperately needed to be over water, but I did.

"Of course." And with that he turned and headed over a beautiful turquoise sea.

It was beautiful and never ending. Now it felt like home to me. Off in the distance there was a small disturbance on the surface of the water. I pointed to it and he turned the machine and flew in that direction. Hovering over the surface at a safe distance, I could see there were whales in the water. I was so excited to know they were here. I looked at them closely and could not really identify the species but it did not matter. Whales had come here and that made me feel safer.

"I do not know what kind of whales they are? They don't look the same as the species we have?" I asked hoping for a explanation.

"They are not any of the species you are familiar with. Many species we have here are compilations of the vast variety of what you experienced in your reality. Some realms here even have species that you are more familiar with from fairy tales. Yes there are realms here that have what you think of as nature spirits. Here you can find most of what you are looking for whether it be in your reality now or not. But you must always remember that no matter which realm you live in, you are still responsible for your environment. If you cannot maintain a predominantly happy existence, your reality can control you in a way that causes a threat to your life." He was always reminding me of that. In truth I guess I needed to be reminded because how my reality worked was so engrained in me, the world in front of me I saw as being an easy one.

"Well what about the children that are born here? Don't they have a huge advantage? It must be easier to be born to it rather than have to learn all of this at an age where learning is not as easy?" I had been wondering about this for a long time, so I decided to ask.

"The answer to that is yes and no. The children that are born here do not have a lot of advantages. They still must learn to to interact with their environment as if it was an extension of themselves. They are not born with any special filters that help them contain their emotions. In some ways it is more difficult because if they do not learn fast enough and they do not have an adult to help them, it is easy for them to fall victim to their environment. Your generation is in the best situation possible. Your people are getting some advance assistance in how to prepare. I would advise you to take advantage of that." He was always a little off when we talked about family and children. Something traumatic had happened to him, and I did not want to pry.

I loved flying over the ocean. It was endless and calming for me. I was born to the sea and from the sea. I could feel my poetic and romantic nature wanting to come out, but this was not the time. We were in a long extended turn now. I knew he was trying to allow me as much ocean as possible before we returned to his home, the jungle. I was grateful for the the glimpse into the future, and knowing there were still whales. It may sound a little odd but I had great faith in whales, and if they were here, it can't be too bad of a place.

After arriving back at the jungle, the clear craft lowered itself back into the cave and almost imperceptibly shut down. At that point the doors opened and we were free to exit. It struck me how the air did not change. I though I would be happy to get that first big breath of fresh air, but it was no different than the air I had been breathing. Although there were no visible vents to transfer the air from the outside, some process had allowed us to breathe constant fresh air. The machine was marvellous and of course I was already wondering how I could get my own when I came here.

"I would love to have one of these machines. Can you tell me anymore about it?" I knew I was probably pushing it, but it never hurts to ask.

"I cannot tell you everything about it, because I do not know. However I do know that it is a living crystalline structure that has almost emotional reactions to the energy it uses to propel itself. So when you saw me touching different symbols, I was sending a slightly different and balancing energy through the skin of the ship. You would think of the skin as the bubble that you see. The ship rides the currents of energy that come from the Earth. Sometimes we will move through an energy that irritates the skin of the ship and that causes a resistance, so another energy must be sent through the skin so there is no resistance. If there is enough resistance it can cause the ship to crash. So an energy is sent through the skin that calms the agitation and removes the resistance. Like I said I do not know all the details but that is the basic premise. I do know however that these skins are grown underground in vast caverns where vortexes move up through them. It conditions them to feed on the energy of the vortex. That somehow prepares them for the propulsion system that is used. Ok enough about that." He walked away from the craft and once again the door sealed itself shut.

We were back on the great lawn now. It was a beautiful day and the air carried the smell of ripening fruit. It made me hungry. Teotihuan offered me a mango. I had mentioned to him long ago that it was my favourite fruit. As I bit into the fruit I thought I felt it express a sense of relief. I immediately removed it from my teeth fearing I had killed it or something. I was quite startled, not sure what to make of it.

Teotihuan laughed at me. "I have been wanting to do that for a long time. The look on your face. I will not forget this moment." he was rolling on the ground unable to contain himself. I couldn't believe it.

He had set me up.

"What is that all about?" The mango now sat on the ground. I was looking at it as if it would start up a conversation with me at any moment.

"Well as you have observed here quite rightly, everything is very alive with both purpose and intent. When you bit into the mango you released its intent and purpose. Its purpose is to nourish others, and its intent is to evolve. However it can only evolve by nourishing others. So you set the mango free and in its gratitude you heard it express itself." It was a lovely and freaky thought to have really. I wasn't sure if I wanted to eat fruit that could tell me I was doing a good job.

"So you are telling me I killed it?"

Teotihuan launched into laughter again. He would go to say something and then put his finger up to say he needed another minute to laugh at me. I am really happy he found it entertaining cause I was not sure what to think.

"I cannot say you killed it. However you did release its essence. So now it is free to become something else. In our world eating fruit, is to honour the essence of the fruit. The fruits greatest desire is to be set free. So it offers itself as nourishment so that we may benefit from its energy as we allow it to become something greater in the process. Eat, eat the fruit. Do not dishonour it now. That is not right. We are in mutual agreement that this is a beautiful merging."

I very cautiously took another bite. This time it was like eating the best mango I had ever tasted fresh off a tree. I did consume it. The taste was almost addictive. When I was finished I could feel the energy of the mango spread through my body. It was living through me. It was experiencing itself as a part of me. I was getting a sense of what it felt it was like to be human because it offered itself to me. It was such an unusual feeling. I could feel the mango and in return it could feel me. I was not sure how to express what I was feeling, but it was most pleasant. I was hoping it was pleasant for the mango as well.

I turned to Teotihuan and sort of raised my shoulders in a gesture that said, "What is happening?"

"You are experiencing the mango and the gratitude it has for you. Express your gratitude for the mango and the cycle will complete itself."

For a very brief moment as I offered gratitude, I could feel the tree that the mango grew on and how it formed and became that mango. I, for just a second, thought I was the mango, and then it was gone. I turned to ask the question but the answer was already on the way.

"You experienced the merging of two energies as they become one. You became the mango and the mango became you. It is how it is here. You experience your reality in a conscious manner. All of it without exception. Do you understand now?" He was smiling as he said this.

Now I understood. This was my final lesson. It is what I needed to really understand everything he had said to me. For a moment I became quite overwhelmed with what that would mean. To experience my reality in a completely conscious manner. I was not sure that was something I could handle. But then again that is what evolution is. We don't grow if we are not challenged. So that was the next step, to be conscious of your life as you live it. Big step.

I was quiet and thoughtful for a few minutes. Teotihuan sat by me with his face to the sun, drinking in the rays as though he were a plant. And then I felt it. We were done. It was like someone suddenly turned everything off and it was silent. I was still there and nothing had changed but everything was different.

"It is over now isn't it?" I asked. My voice was cracking cause I could feel the tears rising in me.

"Yes. It is over. I hope you have enjoyed being here, because I have enjoyed you being here. It is good to see where we have come from and it is also good to see how far we have come. Now however we must continue in preparing others in the same way we have prepared you. We have many to help. We are always accessible to you if you should need us." His voice was calm and reassuring. I hadn't thought about it before, that I was one of many that they were helping. Of course I knew I was not the only person, but I hadn't thought of it in such a way that they were a bit of a revolving door with students coming and going. So I searched my brain to ask him one last question.

"I thank you for this time and this experience. It is all a lot to take in and I will think about this for a long time to come. If I may ask you one more question. I would like to give you the final word if you don't mind. What is the best advice you can leave me with, to prepare for what is to come?" It was all I could think of. I had wanted something grand and life changing. One of those questions that would somehow answer all of the problems in our reality, but advice was all I could think of.

Teotihuan sat back on his hands as he thought about the best way to answer my question. I knew he wanted his words to be right, so he took his time. Then he leaned forward and started to speak.

"Love yourself. Love yourself in a manner that you can carry that love out into the world as a magnet that will draw all to you that need to be loved. Because it is by feeling how you love yourself that they will see it is safe to love themselves as well. Become a self contained unit. By this I mean that you are choosing to consciously create your own reality to the extent you can within the dynamics of your agreed upon reality. Work with your energy field through your body. The path to heaven is through the body, not by denial of it. However you must understand balance of all things. This is why I have given you the processes. They are designed to help you prepare for my reality. They will help you alter your experience and your physical DNA, to encourage the growth of a 5th dimensional body that you can consciously co-create with. But more than anything, Love Yourself."

With that he stood up with outstretched arms. He came forward and hugged me with such strength and love that I was getting light headed. Then when he let go, I could feel myself moving away from him as I watched him get smaller and smaller. All I could do was wave. I was encompassed by the darkness of the void once more. I closed my eyes, forcing the tears from beneath my lids and feeling the sting of the salt. I could feel the bed beneath me, but I did not want to open my eyes. I was not sure I would be going back to Bonampak. If I didn't open my eyes maybe this would not all be happening as it was. However time passes and realty calls. And just like the mango if I do not offer myself to something greater, then I will never know the bliss of growth.

So it is in gratitude that I go forward and offer these words to those that will find them. If you have found these words it is not by chance. If you have found these words you are considering being part of the ascension to the 5th dimension. You may or may not consciously realize it at this point. You may have found these words because you too are being invited to Bonampak. You may also be invited to one of the other realms that are there. It is important now to trust yourself and what you feel. Things in your life are about to become much less easy to explain. Embrace it in joy. Be the mango or be the human it really doesn't matter. In the end we are all one.

Processes and Visualizations

Here all the Processes and Guided Visualizations. You may want to record them in your own voice so it is easier to relax and allow yourself to follow along. Feel free to experiment with the content in these processes. Each one is designed with a specific purpose in mind, but all of them will take you on a journey inside yourself and closer to a 5th dimensional experience. I have placed them here in order for convenience. It can be helpful to keep a journal of what happens during these processes and the changes that occur over time within them. It will tell you a lot about your progress and what is truly going on internally.

Guided Visualization Number One

This visualization is intended to allow you to interact with the memories you have stored in your body. Experiment with Joy and Happiness first. When you feel ready you can recall memories that are not so pleasant to discover where they are anchored in your body. If you wish to disperse the memories that are negative do not place them in your heart and return them to your body. Instead place them in the water and pull the plug and let all the water drain from the tub before you finish the visualization.

Find yourself in a place that is comfortable and quiet. Allow your body to be completely supported by what is beneath you. Breathe deeply. Let you mind relax. Close your eyes and breathe deeply. Relax all your muscles one by one starting with your feet. Relax everything even your scalp and your hair. Now when you are very relaxed I want you to imagine you are in a beautiful bathtub. You have just sunken down into perfectly warmed water. Put some salt in

137

the water so it makes your body feel even more weightless. As you lay back in the tub you can feel the heat moving from your skin into your muscles. The gentle warmth moves deeper and deeper into your body. It cleans and it heals as it goes deeper internally. Soon you are feeling the warmth in the very centre of you body and you are so relaxed you don't want to move. Your body is so comfortable you cannot feel it, all you feel is the warmth and the safety of the salty water.

Now let your mind drift. Let it drift to a place when you were very happy. A moment in time when all that existed was joy. You can feel the happiness spreading throughout your body. It spreads from the centre outwards to your skin. The joy then continues to move outward, moving joyously through your skin and into the water. Allow your joy to tint the water a certain colour. As you do this you can see all the water slowly turning the colour of your joy. You are now floating effortlessly in a tub of warm coloured water. Can you see what colour your joy is? How does the colour feel on your skin? Does the colour have a message for you? Allow the message to gently filter into your thoughts.

Now allow the warm salty water to fully support you in the beautiful tub. Close your eyes and ask your body to allow an image of your joy into your energy field. Feel this image gently form and rise a few inches above your body. Now with your eyes still closed count backwards from 10 to 1. See each number clearly as you count backwards. 10, 9, 8, 7, 6, 5, 4, 3, 2, 1 and then gently open your minds eye. Right in front of you, in your energy field you can see a little hologram of the image of your joy. What is that image? Where is it located on your body? Are there people in the image? If so, who are they? What are you doing in the image? Try to get as much information as you can from the image. When you have as much information as you can get, reach out and hold the image in your hands. Pull the image close to you. Is there anything else you can see now? When you have everything from the image you need, take the image and place it in your heart. Know that this image will gently dissolve within you and send all of its joyous energy through your body.

Now find a spot on your body that needs healing. Allow the colour that is in the water to be drawn towards the spot that needs to heal. Watch as the colour slowly gently moves through the water and into the spot on your body that needs healing. As the warm salty water

138

starts to return to its clear nature you can feel the colour working its magic and spreading throughout your whole body, healing all spots with its joy. Your body is warm and relaxed. You feel whole and complete. Now once again count from 1-10 and when you are ready open your physical eyes and choose to not move too quickly for a few minutes.

Guided Visualization Number Two

In this visualization you will be able to discover how you attach powerful emotions to the words you use. You will also be able to discover why you attached those emotions to those words. This visualization is designed to allow you to take the charge out of words that provoke you. You can also work with this process to assign power to words of your choice. This visualization is about helping you discover how to be in control of the language that you use. This visualization helps to prepare your energy to interact with your surroundings in a physical way. It will allow you to see the affect you have on your environment.

The first thing I want you to do is decide on two words that you would consider to be highly emotional words. Choose 1 positive and 1 negative word. Next I want you to find a comfortable place to be where you won't be disturbed by anything outside of yourself. Settle yourself into a place where you can become totally relaxed. Allow whatever is below you to fully support your body. Breathe deeply and slowly several times to find your centre. Once you feel clear, I want you to close your eyes and imagine you are in a truly magical place. This can be any place that makes you feel like you are limitless. The environment around you loves you and acknowledges your very presence. There may be trees and lakes or maybe you are in a beautiful castle. Choose a place that has magic for you. Allow yourself to be fully present in this space.

Now, interact with the environment around you and it will respond to you. In this space you feel loved by everything, this is your world with no one else to influence it. You are comfortable and relaxed, this space opens it arms to you. You smile and the world around you smiles back.

Slowly now, allow yourself to think of the negative word you chose. Allow it to slowly enter your consciousness. Let yourself feel the word and all the emotions you have attached to it. Go deeper and deeper into the word till the emotion of the word seems to become a physical thing. Allow that emotion to amplify inside of you till you think it is going to explode out of you, then at the last second yell the word into your environment. If you feel safe to do so, you can yell with your voice, if not you can yell in your mind. Make sure you explode every bit of emotional energy out of you in the expression of the word. Your body should feel like you just had a huge release, tired but good. Now slowly without moving your body, use your eyes to explore the direction you yelled in. Look closely at whatever is in front of you. Is there any difference from what was there before? Is there damage? Is anything distorted? Is there a feeling of pain coming from that direction? Use all your senses now to feel what that area felt when you yelled at it. Can you sense what it felt? Is it communicating with you in any way?

Now look deeply into that same area in front of you. Ask yourself why is this word so emotionally charged for me? Focus on wanting to know what event in your life caused you to attach those emotions to that word. Keep looking forward and you will see a mist starting to appear. As the mist grows bigger, you will see an image appear from your past. It may be a snapshot, or it may play like a movie. You may hear words or have strong feelings. Look deeply into the image and remember what was happening in your life at this moment. What you experience now will answer why those emotions are attached to that word. Allow yourself to fully experience this. As long as it is safe, bring it into your body. Remember what you felt. Remember what you heard. Now if you want to change the emotions that are attached to this word, allow yourself to rewrite the scene. Change the scene to what you need it to be so you can attach a different understanding to the word. Once you have rewritten the scene I want you to say the word and attach the new meaning to it, like this, _____ makes me feel _____
Insert the word followed by the emotion you want to feel, then replay the rewritten scene in your mind.

You have now anchored a new emotion to an old word. Now go back to the beginning and rerun the process with your positive word. Take note of how different everything is with the positive emotions anchored to the positive word. Allow yourself to fully experience this difference.

Guided Visualization Number Three

This visualization is designed to allow you to experience the energy portals in your body and the patterns that they hold. You will also discover how these patterns express themselves in your life. You may choose to progress through all the chakra's or you can do them one at a time. In this way you can see the self identity you chose to come here with as opposed to the self identity you project at the moment. This visualization is invaluable if you wish to see the patterns of resistance in your life that can contribute to suffering.

Allow yourself now, to be in a place of rest, relaxation and safety. Let some music play gently in the background if you like. Sit or lay as you prefer. Close your eyes and relax. Breathe deeply and rhythmically. Breathe in and then release the breath slowly. Feel your body release all tensions. You are completely supported by the Universe. Continue to breathe deeply as your body drifts into a deeper state of relaxation. You mind is clearing and getting quiet now. You feel like you are floating on a cloud. You are warm and loved. As you drift into a deeper state of being, you allow yourself to become weightless, you are alert and the distractions of the outside world fade away into the distance as you experience your being in complete relaxation.

As you continue to drift along your awareness slowly, gently starts to focus on your root chakra. Feel the energy moving, spiralling in the colour of red. It is a vibrant strong energy that represents your material possessions, your physical body and your survival. Now focus on how you have manifested these things in your life and mentally make this statement, My soul chose to learn about survival and security through this pattern of belief. You may see images, hear words or have impressions. Allow all the information you need to understand your pattern around survival to come to you now. When you have what you need, release the pattern.

Return to that place of being aware in a relaxed state. Allow yourself now to focus on the second chakra, the sacral chakra. Feel the energy moving, spiralling in the colour of orange. It is a vibrant strong energy that represents your sexuality, your creativity and money. Now focus on how you have manifested these things your life and make this statement, My soul chose to learn about creativity through this pattern of belief. Allow all the information you need to understand your pattern around creativity to come to you now. When you have what you need, release the pattern

Return to that place of being aware in a relaxed state. Allow yourself now to focus on the third chakra, the solar plexus chakra. Feel the energy moving, spiralling in the colour of yellow. It is a vibrant strong energy that represents your personal power, your intellect and your understanding. Now focus on how you have manifested these things in your life and make this statement, My soul chose to learn about power through this pattern of belief. Allow all the information you need to understand your pattern around power to come to you now. When you have what you need, release the pattern.

Return to that place of being aware in a relaxed state. Allow yourself to focus now on the fourth chakra the heart chakra. Feel the energy moving, spiralling in the colour of pink or green. It is a vibrant strong energy that represents love of self and others and forgiveness. Focus on how you have manifested these things in your life and make this statement, My soul chose to learn about love through this pattern of belief. Allow all the information you need to understand your pattern around love to come to you now. When you have what you need, release the pattern.

Return to that place of being aware in a relaxed state. Allow your focus to move to the fifth chakra the throat chakra. Feel the energy moving, spiralling in the colour of sky blue. It is a vibrant strong energy that represents how we voice the truth of our thoughts and feelings and how aligned our head and heart are. Now focus on how you have manifested these things in your life and make this statement, My soul chose to learn about my truth through this pattern of belief. Allow all the information you need to understand your pattern around truth to come to you now. When you have what you need, release the pattern.

Return to that place of being aware in a relaxed state. Allow your

144

focus to move to the sixth chakra the third eye chakra. Feel the energy moving, spiralling in the colour of indigo blue. It is a strong vibrant energy that represents how you see your reality and your intuition. Now focus on how you have manifested these things in your life and make this statement, My soul chose to learn about seeing reality through this pattern of belief. Allow all the information you need to understand your pattern around seeing reality to come to you now. When you have everything you need, release the pattern.

Return to that place of being aware in a relaxed state. Allow your focus to move to the seventh chakra the crown chakra. Feel the energy moving, spiralling in the colour of lavender. It is a strong vibrant energy that represents our connection with Creator. Focus on how you have manifested these things in your life and make this statement, My soul chose to learn about Creator through this pattern of belief. Allow all the information you need to understand your pattern around a Creator to come to you now. When you have all you need, release the pattern.

Return to that place of being aware in a relaxed state. Allow your focus to move to the eighth chakra above your head. Feel the energy moving, spiralling in the colour of white. It is a strong vibrant energy that represents how your physical reality aligns with your soul's purpose. Focus on how you have manifested this in your life and make this statement, My soul chose to learn about itself through this pattern of belief. Allow all the information you need to understand your pattern around your soul's purpose to come to you. When you have all you need, release the pattern.

Allow your understanding to come very clear now about the difference between your true self identity and the identity you wish to be. See how you can make simple changes in your patterns to succeed in doing this. Allow those changes to take place now in your awareness. Bring up two images in front of you, one is the image of your true identity and the other is the image of your desired identity. Look at them both and see how the true identity is starting to fade. It continues to fade until it has completely disappeared. You are now left with your desired identity. Your desired identity starts to move toward you, coming closer and closer. Stretch out your arms to this identity and embrace it. Allow yourself to absorb it completely into your body. Notice how it fits like a glove, you feel so comfortable in this identity. Allow yourself to settle into it as it settles into you. As this happens allow yourself this experience, I am grateful, I am healed, I am loved.

Now slowly start your ascent back to waking reality. Start to hear the sounds around you. Feel the air on your skin. Know that you are about to awaken to a new and wonderful life, and when you are ready open your eyes.

Process Number Four

In this process you will become aware of the patterns that prevent
you from living the life you want. These are the patterns that keep
you from your destiny. Take your time and go slow with this process,
it can be intense especially if you are not accustomed to doing this
kind of work. It is here that you will be able to claim true ownership
of your reality and make the necessary adjustments to sculpt the life
you deserve. It is here where you can be completely honest about
who you are versus who you were taught to be. This process
prepares you to completely own your life, your actions and your
reactions.

Settle yourself into a quiet spot where you know you will not be
disturbed. Have paper and pen handy as you may want to write
things down. Allow yourself to relax and ask that your patterns
clearly come into vision. You may remember some of your patterns
from the last process. Keep them in mind, they may come in handy.
Do a quick scan of your life. Think back as far as you can, right
into childhood if possible. Take note of the memories that pop loudly
into focus. Make note of them. Now bring your focus back to your
current moment. Over the last two years of your life, what has been a
consistent problem for you. Money? Time? Relationships or lack of
relationships? Try to be as specific as you can about the problem.
Such as, if your problem is finding love, say something like this, "I
have been on many dates but no one fits the bill. I am not sure I
believe there are any good men left out there." Or "I work so hard but
I am just making ends meet. I guess I am just not meant to have a
good life."
Once you have written down all the statements you can think of,
read through them. If you have several statements you will start to
see categories emerge. You may have several statements about
money but only a couple of statements about love. You may have

mentioned health several times, while children are only mentioned once. It may help you to match the statements to the categories. The categories should be short, Money, Love, Family, Fear and so on. Now take a look at the statements you have written down. You are looking for similarities in your statements. Most of your statements may be fear based. Perhaps you are angry in most of your statements. Perhaps you find yourself playing the role of victim in your statements. Whatever similarity you find write it down on a separate piece of paper. This is the theme of your negative beliefs.

Now lets move on to something a little cheerier. I want you to look to what is right in your life, what you are happy with, or at least what is ok consistently over the last two years. It could be things as simple as I have great hair, or I finally found a job I like. It could be I just had a baby and I love being a mom. Perhaps something like this, I got dumped two years ago and I was devastated, however it turned out to be the best thing, cause I met someone new and now I am happier than ever.

Follow the same process for these statements, look them over if there are several and see if you can divide them into categories. Place each in its category and then look for similarities in the statements. Find what is similar and when you do turn it into a statement and write it on the same paper you wrote your negative belief theme on.

Now lets look at the stuff in your life that you may do as a hobby or just because you love doing it. Some may be passionate about certain things, others may just have a healthy curiosity. Take a look at your life and ask yourself is there anything you do for pleasure or enjoyment that you have had an ongoing love affair with all your life? Maybe yes or maybe no. If not then ask yourself this question, what would I continue to do in my life even if I was not being paid to do it? Still nothing? Ok well here is my last suggestion. When you allow yourself to daydream about your ideal occupation in life, what are you doing? Describe these things in as much detail as possible. Something like this. When I daydream I see myself on a yacht sailing the ocean. The seas are calm and the food is good. I have a couple of companions with me and I feel safe and happy. We go into every port of call and shop in all the small boutiques by the wharf. We buy all the supplies we need for the next leg of our journey and have a decadent meal before we leave. I never tire of the sunsets, no two are alike. The sound of water moving against the boat lulls me into a beautiful dreamless sleep.

Describe what you see in your imagination with as much emotional and physical detail as possible. Now look through the statements you made about what is right in your life. Again look for any similarities you can find. You may find this in the emotional description or in similarities of what you are doing in your dream and what you are doing that is right in your life. All of these things are clues for you. Write down any similarities you may find and any understandings you may be having about your patterns in this moment. Write it all down because some ideas can be very fleeting.

Now with fresh eyes go back and look at what is wrong in your life. Look at the patterns and beliefs you have discovered that do not make you happy. How different is your dream, from what is wrong in your life? How far apart are your dreams and the things that are wrong in your life? Write down any or all insights you have about your dreams versus your negative patterns.

You should now have a tally of what is not working in your life, what is working in your life and what your dreams are. This is all you need to determine your destiny. Now we are going to ask one last question before we figure out our destiny. Looking at the things that are wrong in your life and the things that are right in your life ask yourself this question. How does it serve my purpose that I have created this polarity in my life?

Here is what I mean. Two ongoing problems I have had in my life are my weight and my finances. Being overweight started in childhood as a way to feel safe in my environment. It was my armour. However as an adult the threats are gone but the weight stayed. Yes it had become a habit, but it had become way more than that. It had become my excuse not to participate in life. It was a great reason to not put myself in situations where I might feel vulnerable or make mistakes. No I did not say I could not do this or that because of my weight, but it was what I was thinking when I turned down many invitations.

Finances were always an issue growing up. There just wasn't any money. When I got old enough to make my own money I found myself to be very driven and I would give it everything I had to make money in minimum wage jobs. I was great at saving and being fugal. But I never had a lot of money. As I got older my finances started to fluctuate even more, having a nice chunk in the bank to being to broke for long periods of time. When I finally had the courage to ask

149

myself what purpose this is serving for me, I realized that I associated money with stress, pressure and the expectation of others. As I got older I was capable of making much more money because I had invested in my talents and had become a very capable person. For me it was a double edged sword. Putting myself out there would mean the money would come, but it would also mean that I would be subject to greater pressure and expectation. Being poor in my eyes, protected me from being vulnerable to the opinions of others. It was also a great reason to not participate in life.

That is when I saw it. I saw the pattern. The things that didn't work in my life didn't work because I as a way to protect myself from vulnerable situations. If you are new to this kind of thinking, this may all sound pretty crazy to you. So I encourage you to ask that question of yourself, :"How does it serve my purpose that I have created this pattern in my life?" Be as honest as you possibly can, no one has to see your answers, only you know the truth. Once again make a list of how these patterns serve you emotionally and look for the common emotion that will emerge from them. This emotion is your hot button. My hot button was vulnerability. Whatever your hot button is, it will play a huge role in your destiny. At this point you may be flooded with memories of this emotion pattern in your life. You may have lots of sudden understandings all at once. This is just confirmation that you hit on the right emotional pattern.

Once you have done this it is time to put it all together. Remember that for this process the definition of destiny is to be able to solve an old ongoing problem in a new way. Once this problem is solved the barriers between what you fear and what you desire can be removed.

So what pattern do you see emerging from the pages you have written on? How does this pattern prevent/protect you from something? Are you ready to release the pattern for good? Are you willing to take the needed steps to release the pattern? Do you feel it is safe for you to release the pattern? Once you have answered all these questions it is time to let go of what no longer serves you.

In the past I have thought that releasing a pattern was as simple as changing my mind about it, seeing it from a different perspective. Sometimes that is very true. I can work for patterns that are not deeply ingrained. For patterns that have been continuously reinforced in your life over decades the process can be a little more involved. For instance, when I was going through the process of discovering my own patterns I started to realize I was walking on my heels. This surprised me because I had always been someone that walked on the ball of my foot. I tried to follow the time line backwards to when it started and I discovered it was initiated during a three year court battle with my ex. It didn't take much to figure out the symbolism. I walked on my heels because I was backing away from life, trying to keep myself safe. I no longer wanted to do that so I consciously started walking on the balls of my feet again. Yes there were a few days of sore muscles just from the adjustment in balance, however I also noticed that I seemed to suddenly become willing to meet things in more of a head on fashion. Walking on the balls of my feet was symbolic for leaning into life, not away from it. That very simple act helped me shift my entire life.

When you are trying to release a pattern it is essential to pay close attention to the details. Little things like how you walk can make a big difference in how successful you will be in achieving your goal. So now you have decided what your pattern is and you are ready to release it, now what do you do? First and most importantly have compassion for yourself. Understand this release may take some time to accomplish and love yourself through it all.

Your emotional hot button is the key to releasing your pattern. Go through your pages till you find your one word emotional hot button. Mine was vulnerability, so we will use it as an example. Once I discovered this was my hot button I started a practice of consistently checking in with myself throughout the day to discover how vulnerable I felt at any given time. On a scale of 1-10 I would rate everything I did throughout the day. I discovered that most things I did that involved other people, made me feel a certain level of vulnerability. If I was in the middle of the bush, I felt safe. With this understanding I was able to define my vulnerabilities even more.

My daily practice was based on two questions, "How vulnerable do I feel in this moment?" And the other question was. How can I make myself feel powerful? Some of the responses I received about how to make myself feel powerful did not always make sense. However I trusted my instincts and followed through. Sometimes they worked and sometimes they didn't. However I did learn how to grow beyond my vulnerabilities. Simply by acknowledging what I felt in the moment I allowed myself to be present enough say, "I was OK." Sometimes that was all it took. As long as there was no threat to life and limb, I was able to tell myself "I am OK, everything is fine."

If you can make a practice of working with yourself in this manner you will teach yourself to see things as they are and not as you are anticipating them to be.

We are all human and all addicted to our habits. If we rush into anything to fast we will just end up replacing one habit for another, or one hot button for another. The most powerful part of this journey is the compassion you must show for yourself. Remember you have been conditioned in this way for years, maybe even decades. It will take a little time and persistence to wean yourself from the pattern, but you can do it, all you have to do, is love yourself through it.

Process Number Five

This process will allow you to begin to communicate with your body in such a way that you will start to perceive it as a co creating partner.

A great way to experience being in your body is by spending time outside with your shoes off. Take the time to ask questions of your body. Ask your feet what they feel when the grass touches them. Ask your skin what it feels when the breeze caresses it. Ask your hair what is feels from the sun. Ask these questions of all parts of your body. You may get some interesting answers, do not dismiss them. Different parts of your body experience reality in different ways. You can also go through the different parts of your body and ask, what emotion lives here. You may find that your nose holds curiosity, while your knees hold intention. Again expect some interesting answers. Take your time to get to know your body. Start treating it as though your life depends on the partnership you create with it, because you know what, it does. But most of all, be kind, be compassionate and be accepting. You are the only you that has ever been on this planet. Never before and never again will there be another you, and I believe that is pretty special and pretty powerful. Treat yourself like you believe it too.

Make sure you are participating in your life. Life can get crazy and it is easy to lose focus. Every now and then try to take a minute and think about the last week of your life. How much of it did you do for you? Did you spend all your time taking care of other people's needs? Did you do nothing but work? Don't try to justify it to yourself that work is not about someone else. Come on, really? If it really was for you and you loved it so much you wouldn't classify it as work would you? Just try to make sure every week you take some time and put you in your life. While you are doing that, you may as well be fully in your body experiencing reality and that way you can kill two birds with one stone. If you need to be addicted to something, then being aware of your body would be a good thing to develop into a habit. Just think of what you could accomplish if you were aware of what you were doing all the time. Life is meant to be enjoyed for the most part. If you are not participating in your life, then you are not enjoying the life you are in. Give yourself permission to tweek your life just a little. Tweek it enough to put a smile on your face everyday, that is all it will take.

Visualization Number Six

This process allows you to anchor yourself to your body. It also allows you to learn how to project your energy to a desired spot and to retrieve energy from a desired spot. It helps you become aware of consciously moving your energy around from point to point and how it feels to do this. It also teaches you about your own symbolism and how you interpret different energies.

Calm and centre yourself. Allow yourself to relax. Breathe deeply. Close your eyes. Now I want you to form an image in your mind of what you think it would look like if you had a spot in your body where you anchored yourself. The image could be anything as long as it represents security, solidity and safety to you. Once your body is relaxed and you feel calm and present, allow your awareness to slowly move down through your body. In all of us there is a point where we anchor ourselves into our physical bodies. As you move your awareness down through your body pay attention to how it feels. Where you are warm and where you are cold. What parts are easy to move through and what parts are challenging. Move down through your body from one end to another. Now go back to where you started and set your intention to find the anchor point in your body. Once again bring your awareness to your body and slowly move from one end to the other looking for the image you saw earlier that represented your anchor. When you find the spot that holds your anchor, stop and move into that spot. Take some time and explore this spot. How does it feel to you? Is it hard or soft? Is it warm or cool? What colour is it? Does this spot have a name? How do you feel about this spot? Where is the spot located in your body? Are there any memories attached to this spot? When you are finished exploring this spot, just sit with it and thank it for being the safe anchor that it is. This is the place inside of you that you can retreat to if you need to feel safe. This is where you are anchored into your body. It is also the spot you can launch yourself from to anchor yourself in other places. Look at your anchor now. If you look very closely you will see a small door that opens. Inside this door is the method to attach yourself to another spot. It could be a rope, roots or a bungee cord, but whatever it is, it will open a pathway to another place for you to anchor your energy. Now think of somewhere you would like to anchor yourself, perhaps a star or the moon, or maybe the source energy itself. Get a clear image in your mind of what your destination is then remove your line of energy from its container. Now with your intention firmly in mind take the line of energy and throw it will all your might watching it land and anchor itself at its intended destination. As soon as it is anchored it starts to send energy to you. You can feel the energy coming to you and filling your body. You can feel yourself getting calmer and stronger. You can feel this loving energy move through every cell allowing you to be solidly in your physical body. You are present, your are calm, you are congruent. Allow yourself to become completely grounded by this new energy. Once you are full, allow the line of energy between you and your destination to retract itself back into the anchor in your body. Close the door on the anchor and allow yourself to expand your awareness through your whole body once again. As you do this you may want to offers thanks for the new energy. You may want to feel gratitude and marvel at how miraculous the universe is. And now say thank you to yourself for all that you do and all that you have to offer. As you send love outward also send it inward. As you are ready open your eyes.

Visualization Number Seven

This Visualization allows you to hear the Whispers from your Eight Rooms. It allows you to connect to your own truth. I allows you to see who participates in this reality with you. This process will also allow you to see how your energies are changing and preparing for the ascent into the 5th dimension. By comparing what you discover during this process to what is traditionally known about the chakra's, you will discover how your body is individually adapting to the incoming 5th dimensional energies. Again, feel free to adapt this visualization. Change or add more questions as your need for information changes. This is a flexible process which you can use to monitor your progress as our reality changes. You may want to record this one as well for an enhanced experience.

Find a comfortable spot. Release your body to the support that is beneath it. Breathe deeply and rhythmically. In and out, in and out, till you can feel yourself relax. Relax all parts of your body. Make sure you will not be disturbed and continue breathing deeply. Allow yourself to start feeling distant from your body. Allow yourself to know that your are ready to know more. Close your eyes and breath deeply. Follow the gentle rhythm of your breath, in and out, in and out. Now you are totally relaxed and feeling like you are floating gently just above your body. You are still very connected to your body but not confined by it. Continue to breathe deeply. Now as you are in a state of complete relaxation, give yourself permission to have full knowing of your eight rooms.

The first room of your life is your room of survival. Gently hold the idea of survival in your mind and move through your body. Allow yourself to find the spot where your survival is located in your body. When you find it, look at it very carefully. What does it look like? Is there anyone in that room? Who is it? What colour is the

157

room? How big is it? Is it clean or messy? Can you see yourself in that room? Does something appear to be missing in the room? If so, what? On the other side of the room is a window, open it and look out, you will see what you need for your survival. When you have finished exploring your room of survival, allow yourself to heal whatever may need healing in that room, and when you are finished send love to the room and and bring your consciousness back to the centre.

The second room of your life is connections. Gently hold the idea of connections in your mind and allow your consciousness to move through your body and find this room. Allow yourself to find the spot where your connections is located in your body. When you find it, look at it very carefully. What does it look like? Is there anyone in that room? Who is it? What colour is the room? How big is it? Is it clean or messy? Can you see yourself in that room? Does something appear to be missing in the room? If so, what? On the other side of the room is a window, open it and look out, you will see what you need for your connections. When you have finished exploring your room of connections, allow yourself to heal whatever may need healing in that room, and when you are finished send love to the room and and bring your consciousness back to the center.

The third room of your life is your power. Gently hold the idea of power in your mind and allow your consciousness to move through your body and find this room. Allow yourself to find the spot where your connections is located in your body. When you find it, look at it very carefully. What does it look like? Is there anyone in that room? Who is it? What colour is the room? How big is it? Is it clean or messy? Can you see yourself in that room? Does something appear to be missing in the room? If so, what? On the other side of the room is a window, open it and look out, you will see what you need for your power. When you have finished exploring your room of power, allow yourself to heal whatever may need healing in that room, and when you are finished send love to the room and and bring your consciousness back to the centre.

The fourth room of you life is your love. Gently hold the idea of love in your mind and allow your consciousness to move through your body and find this room. Allow yourself to find the spot where your connections is located in your body. When you find it, look at it very carefully. What does it look like? Is there anyone in that room? Who is it? What colour is the room? How big is it? Is it clean or messy? Can you see yourself in that room? Does something appear to be missing in the room? If so, what? On the other side of the room is a window, open it and look out, you will see what you need for love. When you have finished exploring your room of power, allow yourself to heal whatever may need healing in that room, and when you are finished send love to the room and and bring your consciousness back to the centre.

The fifth room of your life is your truth. Gently hold the idea of truth in your mind and allow your consciousness to move through your body and find this room. Allow yourself to find the spot where your connections are located in your body. When you find it, look at it very carefully. What does it look like? Is there anyone in that room? Who is it? What colour is the room? How big is it? Is it clean or messy? Can you see yourself in that room? Does something appear to be missing in the room? If so, what? On the other side of the room is a window, open it and look out, you will see what you need for truth. When you have finished exploring your room of power, allow yourself to heal whatever may need healing in that room, and when you are finished send love to the room and and bring your consciousness back to the centre.

The sixth room of your life is your perception. Gently hold the idea of perception in your mind and allow your consciousness to move through your body and find this room. Allow yourself to find the spot where your connections is located in your body. When you find it, look at it very carefully. What does it look like? Is there anyone in that room? Who is it? What colour is the room? How big is it? Is it clean or messy? Can you see yourself in that room? Does something appear to be missing in the room? If so, what? On the other side of the room is a window, open it and look out, you will see what you need for perception. When you have finished exploring your room of power, allow yourself to heal whatever may need healing in that room, and when you are finished send love to the room and and bring your consciousness back to the centre.

The seventh room of your life is your reception. Gently hold the idea of reception in your mind and allow your consciousness to move through your body and find this room. Allow yourself to find the spot where your connections is located in your body. When you find it, look at it very carefully. What does it look like? Is there anyone in that room? Who is it? What colour is the room? How big is it? Is it clean or messy? Can you see yourself in that room? Does something appear to be missing in the room? If so, what? On the other side of the room is a window, open it and look out, you will see what you need for reception. When you have finished exploring your room of power, allow yourself to heal whatever may need healing in that room, and when you are finished send love to the room and and bring your consciousness back to the centre.

The eighth room of your life is your Oneself. Gently hold the idea of the Oneself in your mind and allow your consciousness to move through your body and find this room. Allow yourself to find the spot where your connections is located in your body. When you find it, look at it very carefully. What does it look like? Is there anyone in that room? Who is it? What colour is the room? How big is it? Is it clean or messy? Can you see yourself in that room? Does something appear to be missing in the room? If so, what? On the other side of the room is a window, open it and look out, you will see what you need for the Oneself. When you have finished exploring your room of power, allow yourself to heal whatever may need healing in that room, and when you are finished send love to the room and and bring your consciousness back to the centre.

Now allow yourself to remember all the details you need to know to make positive changes in your life. Slowly allow yourself to become aware of your body. You are light and happy and when you are ready, open your eyes.

For more information please contact:

Rose McMullen

taonow1@hotmail.com

www.rosemcmullen.com

https://www.facebook.com/rose.mcmullen.33

https://www.facebook.com/ancientteachings